Vulnerability
as the Road to
Change

Vulnerability
as the Road to

Change

PRATIMA NAGARAJ

Happy Publishing

VULNERABILITY AS THE ROAD TO CHANGE

Copyright © 2015, Pratima Nagaraj
Foreword by Dr. Dain Heer

Cover photo by Rita Jayaraman
Margo Rita Photography, Singapore

Cover Design by Melinda Asztalos
Interior Design & Typography by Roseanna White Designs

Published by Happy Publishing, www.HappyPublishing.net

First Edition
ISBN: 978-0-9896332-5-3

I dedicate this book to the two
most incredibly amazing men I know—
my husband Nagaraj
and Dr. Dain Heer,
Co-Creator of Access Consciousness®
who have inspired me to be more vulnerable
and choose more of me every single day.
I am extremely grateful for their presence in my life.

*T*able of *C*ontents

PART FOUR
The 30-Day Vulnerability Challenge

Foreword

By Dr. Dain Heer,
Co-Creator, Access Consciousness®

Imagine if you had one person in your life that unconditionally cared for you and that didn't judge you–ever. If you have one, or if you could imagine having one, what would it be like to be in their presence? It would most likely give you a sense of peace, a sense of space, and a sense of ease, maybe even erasing years of self-judgment and self-recrimination by the space of no judgment that they were willing to be.

Can you even begin to imagine it? If you can, this book will give you the inspiration and the practical tools to create it. If you can't just yet, this book will give you the inspiration to start seeking that. It asks you to examine your life and find what is true for you, and most of all, it invites you to *like* you again.

The author of this book, Pratima Nagaraj, has a level of courage that has allowed her to walk the precarious path to truly having her.

Along the way, she had to question what her culture enforced as true, what her family said was true, and in so doing find what was actually true for her. And what emerged was not a selfish, unkind, uncaring person, but instead a truly caring being that no longer had to hide the intensity of caring that she has for others or herself.

I'm going to bet that you'll be able to perceive the caring that Pratima has for you and the concurrent courage she has to choose for her, as you read the pages of this book.

Pratima is inviting you to experience true vulnerability with yourself, something that we have all been told has no value in the reality we live in, and yet, it is exactly that which, if you have the courage to embrace it, will give you *you* in a way that has never been possible before.

I am honored to be her friend, and I am greater for the caring she has for me. And the world is greater for the caring she has for it.

PART

One

New Beginnings

Writing this book has fundamentally changed my life. It has taught me to be vulnerable at a completely different level. I had to find the words to describe what I am aware of energetically and that's always been very challenging. Writing was always a distant dream for me, as it can take me hours to form one sentence. This book has taken me on an interesting inward journey and it has taken me into depths of myself that I had never accessed before. It brought to my cognitive awareness a lot of things that I was only aware of at an energetic level. Writing this book has also helped me unlock and discover my capacities with translating energy into words so that vulnerability can be presented to you, the reader. It has taken me a great deal of courage and vulnerability to write on a topic that's considered not easy and common, and then get the book published so you could see this. It feels like choosing to walk outside naked. That's exactly what I am exploring and advocating for in this book and I love the fact that I get to walk my talk.

I avoided writing this for a few months, but the book

was extremely clear that it wanted to be written and shine brightly for you. It has a life of its own and it was given to me to honor this. The voice was getting louder every single day and it reached a point where I couldn't ignore it anymore and I had to get to work! Giving birth to this book has been one of the most fun, joyful, exhilarating and fulfilling experiences of my life so far and I know the book has a life and consciousness of its own and creates whatever it desires to create. To me, even if one person reads this book and gets to see the world differently, be more of themselves and be comfortable in their own skin, then that is success. I wonder what else is possible.

The fact that you were drawn to pick up this book and you are reading about this topic shows that you already are aware of the energy of vulnerability in you and your life. You know what it is, may not be cognitively, otherwise you probably wouldn't be reading this! I am excited that we will be together exploring what it is to choose vulnerability.

Before you even begin to read this book, you might already have known, read, told or sold information about what vulnerability is from family, friends, books, movies, culture, religion, society, spiritual groups or metaphysics. You probably have existing definitions, meanings and points of views of what vulnerability is or isn't, just like I did before I started to explore this. What worked for me was my willingness to let go of everything I had learned and being open to looking at what is different? What else is possible that I haven't considered? It reminds me of a story of the Zen master and a Buddhist scholar. The scholar who had an extensive background in Buddhist studies and was an expert in his area, went to see the Zen master one day. They sat in a kitchen together and the scholar rambled about how knowledgeable he was and his extensive doctrinal background. The master listened to him patiently and began to make his tea. He poured the tea into the scholar's cup until it began to overflow and run all over the floor. The scholar noticed and shouted "Stop! The cup is full, you can't get any more in". The master stopped pouring and said "You are like this cup. You are full of ideas and beliefs and your cup is full. Unless you empty your cup, you cannot add fresh tea into it".

This story is an old one but it gives an interesting message. We are so enamoured by our opinions, beliefs and fixed points of views that we buy into from everyone and everything around us and so trapped by our own conditioning that we fill ourselves up to the brim and nothing else can get in, that doesn't match our already existing judgments. What if instead, we could be in the question of "What else is possible that I haven't yet considered?" at all times. Never concluding what is right or wrong and always open to exploring new horizons that give you access to unlimited possibilities.

Barriers. Walls. Defences.

What if we could dissolve all of them?

What if we can start being present and live every moment of our lives to the fullest?

Here is an invitation to a radically different possibility with vulnerability!

How Access Consciousness®
Changed My Life

All my life I knew something different was possible than what exists. When I looked at this reality, the people around me, family, friends etc., I knew I did not fit in. I was very different. I had made this difference of me a wrongness. I judged myself, made everything and everyone outside of me greater than me and lived with a sense of inadequacy. Having lived my life based on this premise, I went on to create an un-fulfilling corporate career, unhappy, unsuccessful, frustrated relationships and an unhealthy body that drove me into seeking a different way of life. Like most people, I went into spirituality and metaphysics, which gave me respite for a couple of years. But very soon a different kind of discontentment kicked in. What I thought would empower me, on the contrary, made me more dependent on spiritual teachers. I kept looking for answers and it was never ending. I was asking the universe to lead me to something different and demanded that things change very soon.

That's when I came across Access Consciousness®, founded by Gary Douglas and co-created by Dain Heer. I went for my first Access Bars® session, four years back, very reluctant and sceptical. I remember asking my therapist, "How much can I release and change in these 90 minutes?" She, very nonchalantly replied "As much as you would like to let go and change".

It pissed me off because I knew that the ball was in my court now. I couldn't blame her if the session didn't work as it was my choice to choose the amount of change I desired. Deep down I was excited because for once someone gave me the permission to choose change to whatever extent I desired, without saying I had to take 10 sessions before things can change. After 90 minutes of getting my Bars run, I got up from the table feeling very light and happy and nothing seemed like a problem anymore! Cognitively I had no clue what had changed, but energetically I felt absolutely fantastic. I asked her what else can I explore from there and she handed me the book "*Being You, Changing the World*" by Dain Heer.

As I read the book, I felt as if it was customized for me. Everything that Dain Heer talked about in the book made so much sense to me and I felt like I knew all of it already. No one had ever put it across in a way that he did, which was truly empowering. This book was an invitation for me to explore more of the tools of Access Consciousness® which completely transformed my life four years back and still continues to do so every single day.

When I started using the tools of Access, my constant quest for answers ended and for the first time in my life I experienced true empowerment. The rapidity of change I noticed was mind blowing. It was a wakeup call and it shattered my life the way I had known. All the lies, judgments and fixed beliefs I had created about me and my life were gone. There was more space and possibility now to create my life the way I truly wanted. There was also a huge sense of relief and freedom in my world as I didn't have to look up to anyone outside of me for answers, not even Gary and Dain. All I had to do was ask questions and receive the awareness. It truly has empowered me to know that I know! I can't thank Gary Douglas enough for creating the tools of Access Consciousness® and changing the lives of millions of people around the world, including mine. He shows us that a different world can exist, one full of ease, happiness and infinite possibilities. I am not surprised that Access Consciousness® is now present in 170+ countries and I wonder what would it take for everyone on this planet to have these tools of empowerment? I wish I had these tools when I was born. I would have created my life in a completely different way!

Chapter 1

What Is Vulnerability?

When I came across the word 'vulnerability' and I heard Gary Douglas, founder of Access Consciousness® and Dain Heer, co-creator of Access Consciousness®, talk about choosing to be more vulnerable a few years back, I thought it was bizarre and unusual. My first thought was "Why would someone want to choose more weakness, be hurt or be emotionally exposed?" This is what I had known about vulnerability until then. That's how I understood it. Usually when I come across a new word, the first thing I do is look it up in a dictionary, or if there is someone around me, ask them about what it means. This was my initial learning of what vulnerability was, years ago. I also looked it up in the dictionary and this is how dictionaries define vulnerability:

- *Able to be easily physically, emotionally, mentally hurt, influenced or attacked*

- *Exposed to the possibility of being attacked or harmed, physically or emotionally*

- *Susceptible to emotional injury*

- *Open to censure or criticism*

When I asked people around me as to what's their first thought when they hear the word 'vulnerability' the most common responses were: Weakness, being in a defenseless position, being a doormat, open to threat, to be taken advantage of, being open to criticism, scary, emotional exposure, shame, fear, and so forth.

This is how we usually create associations. Each word above has an energy to it. Can you sense it? Every time I read the above definitions, it makes me feel heavy and contracted, as if a big fat elephant is sitting on my head! One of the key tools I have learned from Access Consciousness® is that what is true for you makes you feel light, and what is heavy is a lie. So it is obvious there is a lie attached in the above definitions – as they feel very heavy. Every time we use words based on the definitions that we have learned or bought from someone or something else, we are creating exactly that energy in our life.

Having used the word vulnerability synonymously with weakness, I was curious to explore what Gary and Dain had to say differently. They busted all the myths and misconceptions I had created around this and I am very grateful to them for showing me a different possibility which has truly transformed my life.

For as long as I can remember, I have been (and I believe people collectively have been) buying into the myth that vulnerability is weakness and thus is something negative. There are several myths and misconceptions about what being vulnerable is and its impact and importance in our lives. It is often confused with wearing emotions on the sleeve or allowing other people to indiscriminately know about your deepest darkest secrets and emotions. Displaying all your emotions on a table for everyone who walks by to see, is not what vulnerability is all about. We see being vulnerable as opening a Pandora's Box from which we want to protect ourselves, but in that process we forget that's the path that leads to finding and expressing who we really are.

HAVING NO BARRIERS/DEFENSES

What if vulnerability is very different from what you think it is? What if it is about breaking out of your self-imposed barriers and taking off the armours you put around you so that you are not open to the world? What if it is not weakness, but on the contrary, it's your willingness to be courageous enough to be the way you are, be comfortable in your own skin without having the need to create any masks or pretend that you are someone you are not. What if it means you have the courage to expose yourself to the world as you are and receive the judgments or criticisms that can come your way in that process.

Real vulnerability is being without any barriers or walls around you, not living in a confinement of rules, defenses and belief systems that you have created; and being open to receive and accept everything that shows up in your life without judging it as right, wrong, good or bad. You will not resist it or oppose it, you will not stand in the way of it. You can be like a rock in a stream of water. You simply allow everything to flow and accept its existence in totality.

The purpose of the barriers that we build is to avoid being vulnerable. These walls either keep us locked in to something or keep us from accessing something. When you embody vulnerability you no longer have the "need" for these walls. It's just a matter of choice - whether you want to have it or not. Does having it work for you or does it not? You don't have to build walls as an automatic response anymore.

"You are confined only by the walls you build yourself."

OPEN TO RECEIVING

Vulnerability has been misconstrued as weakness and being hurt. It's not. But if that's what you believe, then being vulnerable is a bad thing, something to be avoided at all costs. At first it may even sound realistic and good. It may sound like a desire to live our lives without pain, suffering or being hurt. Isn't that something we all ask for? But have you considered how much energy and effort you have to use in order to block all of this from your life by putting up barriers to it, which in turn cuts off your ability to receive things, to a large extent? These barriers are not smart, they don't know what to block and what not to, so they prevent a lot of good things coming into your life too, like money and happiness! So when you live within these barriers and you opt not to break out of it, you are not only stopping things from coming into your lives, but you are suffocating in the confines, cooking in your own beliefs and judgments. Now, that doesn't seem like a smart choice, does it?

Having Total Awareness

If you haven't heard the mantra of Access Consciousness® it says "*All of life comes to me with ease, joy and glory*"® ALL OF LIFE includes the good, bad and the ugly. What if you can be open to receiving all of life, which includes the pain and suffering, and yet it comes to you with total ease and joy? In this way you are not resisting or blocking anything and you are not being the effect of it either.

One of the key aspects of vulnerability is to live without any barriers. When you are completely open, it is true that you risk being hurt and you will become more aware of the pain and suffering of everyone around you – even if they are thousands of miles away, simply because we are all like psychic radars receiving information from everything around us all the time. But with this risk, there comes a great level of awareness. You get to see how people around you are functioning, what choices they are making, what judgments they have about you and themselves and so on. You can then choose to either get hurt or look at what you are receiving as just a piece of information and allow it to flow. At least you haven't blocked your awareness and you have all the information you require to make a different choice that works for you. You are in charge here and no one else can control your life when you are this way.

People assume that if they are vulnerable they will be taken advantage of and stomped into dust. So they feel they have to erect boundaries that create a line of protection around them. These boundaries can be any kind of a defense system or something that you believe in strongly; a fixed point of view that you have or just plain resistance. It can be tricky because these things are invisible and very ingrained in you, so there are times you don't even know they exist. These invisible walls limit your sense of perception and the amount of information that can reach you. When you are in your defenses, you cannot know what the other person is thinking or doing. Instead, if you dissolve these boundaries and be open, you can receive all the information about the person. Are they cheating on you? Are they backstabbing you? Are they manipulating you? Being mean? Judging you? You get my point. Once you have all information, you can then choose to do what works best for you. You can also use it to your advantage.

I'd like to give a real life example here. I was working with someone as part of my business and we would work together very often. I used to always feel heavy, cranky and low in energy when I was around this person, and I made myself small and less. I knew there was something about this person I resisted, but I didn't know what it was. Do you notice that's a barrier I had there that prevented me from having the awareness? I knew I wanted things to change desperately and nothing was working until I chose to be vulnerable with this person. I lowered all my barriers and let the awareness flow in. It was very intense to begin with as it was a huge amount of information that I had blocked for many months which came in like a Tsunami. (I want to take a side step and point this out here, that when you dissolve those boundaries, you may feel like things are getting more intense. That's because you are now receiving all the information easily which you had blocked until then. So things are not actually getting worse, you are just more aware now).

My instant reaction to avoid this intensity was to bring those walls up and block it, but I consciously chose not to. I was willing to see the truth. I wanted to see it all, as I knew that's the only way things can change. I kept my barriers down and it took me few hours to realize that this person was judging the hell out of me, trying to control me, manipulate me, and was being a superior asshole. The more I resisted it, the easier it was for this person to do more of it.

I chose something different now that I had this information. I no longer functioned from blind faith and trust that this person was my awesome friend and cannot be or do this. I was willing to see the truth and receive all these judgments without buying into them as real and true. I stopped judging me and playing small because I realized none of that was mine in the first place. I was just picking up on this person's judgments of me. I was now willing to stand up for me, put my foot down and didn't let this person mess with me anymore. Because I had no resistance, I could not be controlled by them anymore. There were times when I knew exactly what this person would say or do and I could manipulate them or use the situation to my advantage. It got easier to work together and I didn't have to give up being ME or pretend to be someone I am not, in order to do that.

So even if there is someone wanting to attack you, if you are truly being vulnerable and living with no confines, you allow yourself to receive this information ahead of time so that you can either plan to run, call for help, or do something else to change the situation. We assume that having barriers give us protection but on the contrary, I have heard Gary Douglas say this repeatedly, that vulnerability is your greatest form of protection and insurance, even in the face of danger. I am slowly beginning to understand how this works!

"What vulnerability could you embrace today, that would allow you to create the change that you are asking for?"

BEING SEEN AND HEARD, BEING YOU

What happens when you live without barriers or walls? You will be seen, obviously! You are unable and not wanting to hide anything about you from this world anymore. That may not sound good, initially. Being seen and known may be equated to being judged, criticized or being hurt, based on past associations and beliefs you might have held. That's how it was for me.

So I tried all my life to hide myself in a box so that I am not seen. I believed I could avoid judgments and being hurt this way. That's a tad bit insane, I agree, but hey we all do insanity in our own ways, don't we? I used to think that when people know me well, that would give them the ability to influence me, judge me or control me. Then a few instances I've come across strengthened these beliefs – a family member or someone close to me and knows about my past failures, brings them up in a public conversation; a friend knows a secret and shares it with others, resulting in embarrassment and a public joke; a partner knows about your insecurities and uses it to control you or win an argument.

I had made these things very significant and let them rule my life. I now know that these reasons are not good enough to block everything and limit oneself. These were some of the instances in my life when I had learned to hide myself. All of us have certain defining moments in our lives where we learn to do this, in different ways. Before you go ahead, take a moment to see when and where you learned to hide you. Was it as early as when you were five years old or even earlier? Part of this exploration process is to become aware of these moments, recognize what you did there, and what would you have liked to do different then? Imagine now that you are doing it differently. It's like re-writing your story. It may sound very simple, but it shifts the energy around it, removes the emotional charge and gives you the freedom to create your life differently. You no longer create the same pattern, on an auto-pilot mode, based on these past events. We assume that there have to be complex solutions to our problems but more often than not, these simple choices create powerful changes.

It is true that you have to have the willingness to be open but that does not mean you share everything with everyone. It is not unloading your life onto people nor is it the constant need to share. Before you say something to somebody, you have to ask (in your head) what that other person is willing to hear and receive and tell them exactly that much. Not more. Not less. What it does is, it removes the "I need protection" as a reason to hide yourself and not be open. Instead you can live from awareness and choice. Can you sense how much freedom the latter option gives you? It's time to choose that now!

"Your real self is one of the greatest gifts you can give to yourself and to this world."

When I am being this way, like an open book, people are able to access the real ME, the true being, the core essence of what I am. They see the genuineness in who I am and they can sense that I am comfortable in my own skin. Over the past six months, more and more people have come up to me to say that they are able to connect with me better and that they feel included in my world. I've been able to establish better relationships and connections with people too, and it is much more fulfilling than doing it wearing a mask or pretending to be who I am not.

"If you didn't have to hide you, who would you be and what would you choose?"

"Who, what, when, where and how would you be if you gave up all your pretenses?"

When you are not vulnerable – when you create armours for defense and protection, when you hold onto what is right for you, when you have the need to act and pretend who you are not, you are limiting possibilities in your life. When you are vulnerable, you open the doorways to unlimited possibilities. When you are pretending to be vulnerable, people around you can sense that it is false and you are faking it, and they are not going to be interested in what you have to say or offer to them.

SPEAKING YOUR TRUTH, BEING HONEST

Being vulnerable is about honoring your truth and voicing it out, and not having the need to suppress it or hide it from you or anyone else. If you have a preference, speak up. If you need help, ask for it. If you want to cry, do it. It's about never holding back anything or worrying about what others will think about you if you express your emotions. There are times when you need to speak your truth, for yourself, regardless of how it is received and whether someone understands it or not.

To be vulnerable, you must first be completely honest with yourself. To avoid feeling weak if you resort to stuffing down your feelings, repressing and suppressing them to a point of numbness – then you reach a state where you cannot recognize yourself and you have to figure out how to deal with the mess you created. It took me a great deal of brutal honesty with myself to get to where I am today. I had to acknowledge that I have gifts as well as limitations and it is completely OK to show it all to the world. Most importantly, to see myself in this light. There was no need to hide it or stifle myself by burying it. I was ready to face it, deal with it and change it all. I know I am not perfect and I don't have to be seen as perfect.

Perfectionism is a judgment. If you have never pondered that, I encourage you to look at it right now because many of us get stuck with the need to be perfect. Perfectionism comes with what is right or wrong and anything that has the duality of right or wrong, good or bad, and is a judgment. When I was honest with myself, I no longer had to be stuck with the shackles of perfectionism. I no longer had to hide my flaws, deny parts of me that I labelled as negative, bad or imperfect. I am ready to have an unedited and unfiltered version of me out in the world!

"How much fun could you have if you didn't have to be perfect?"

Choosing this was a huge step for me and it did seem scary, but the truth is, fear and excitement feel exactly the same way, physiologically. So what if it is not fear that you are feeling, but it is actually the excitement of the possibilities that this choice will open up for you? Once I got the point of view that fear is not real, that fear is something we choose as a way of distracting ourselves from seeing our potential, I was excited to explore what this awareness would create for me. I understand that you may feel the uncertainty, initially, as to how people will receive the "real you" when you put yourself out there in the open or you might wonder what will show up when you speak your truth. More often than not, that uncertainty is the place where exciting opportunities and an alternate way of life exists. That's where the change that we keep asking for resides. That's what we avoid in the name of fear.

PART Two

MY JOURNEY
TO VULNERABILITY

Chapter 2

It's Just a Choice

I come from India, a country that has a conservative culture compared to the rest of the world and also from a family with very orthodox and traditionalistic values. Being the only child to my parents, I was raised in a very protective way. I learned from a very young age that 'I need to protect myself', especially being a female. It was an automatic response system to put up barriers around me, as I believed that having barriers would keep me safe and secure.

That's how most of us function, don't we? This continued all my life – during school, at work, in friendships and romantic relationships. Little did I know at that point that I was functioning from a lie? The truth is that these barriers of protection that we create actually block our awareness of people and the environment around us. We are then literally walking around being unaware. When we are unaware, it is more likely that we will fall into trouble than not. Instead, if you actually choose to be vulnerable, and not resist any information that is around you, both cognitively and energetically, you are completely aware of everyone and everything. So even if there is a possibility that someone could attack you, you have that information now and you would either not be in that place at that time or make a different choice to change the situation. Have you ever felt in your life that you have been at the right place at the right time? Well, those are the times when you have been vulnerable and were willing to have the awareness of everything so knew you had to be there, and things will fall into place, even if it that awareness wasn't cognitive.

While growing up, I had an intense need to please everyone around me and get people to like me. I could not stand it if someone would get upset with me, didn't want to talk to me or just disliked me, with a valid reason or not! That was good enough for me to go into the judgment of myself, a place I visited very often or at times lived there for days and weeks. Clearly, handling rejection was not my cup of tea. I sucked at it. Seeking approval and validation from people was how I saw and defined my self-worth. Not surprised that I ended up having relationships with people who rejected me more and more and I allowed them to walk all over me. Little did I realize that the one person who was rejecting me the most was ME. I had created barriers to my own self, which was nourished and cemented over years to make it stronger, so much so that I had no inkling of who I truly was. I didn't recognize the fact that everything I was seeking from others, was something I was not willing to gift to myself and be for myself. This realization dawned on me a few decades late though!

Looking back at my life, I can now see that I was extremely aware and vulnerable as a kid and I would not have any filters when I talked to people, which included adults. I was told that I was too straight forward, too loud, too much, too bold, etc. I was made wrong for being that. I didn't fall into the category of "good" and "obedient" kids. Most of my friends and relatives disliked me and I would always be the odd one out, be it in school or at home.

So in order to not feel left out and to "fit in" with them, I did things that would make people happy, even if it meant that it would make me extremely frustrated and unhappy. It felt like I gradually cut off parts of me and started losing my essence, the connection with me, in order to create an image and be that person people would like. This way of life continued over years as I grew up and I continued to choose it in all my relationships – romantic, personal and at work. I couldn't say "no" to people because I wanted to please them.

I would end up with tasks that I didn't want to do, and in relationships that I didn't want to be in. Why am I saying all this? Because I know it is not just me on this planet who does this. We all have given up ourselves for some weird reasons and created a 'public' image that we put on, the moment we step out of our cozy bedroom. I would only get a glimpse of who I was when I stayed in solitude. I knew that was not all. There were other aspects of me, like my talents and abilities, the good, bad and ugly that I had hidden very well – so deep, even from myself. I finally made a choice to be more vulnerable and look at myself with total love, kindness and caring as I would have for a new born baby. It was then that I saw those walls slowly melt and disappear, giving access to the real me.

As I've dived deeper into this inward journey in the past

year, I've understood the true power of vulnerability a lot more – it is for our personal growth. It is imperative for us to deeply know and find ourselves. The more vulnerable I am, the better I am able to connect with people, both personally and professionally. It's easier because there are no barriers creating the separation. I've had many friends and clients come up to me recently to say how they find me very different. They feel included in my world, they find me softer and gentler and easy to approach and above all that they are happy to be around me.

Have you ever interacted with someone who is pretending to be who they are not? They were putting up a fake appearance in such a way that they almost came across as pseudo and hollow and you could see through them that they were not being real?

- How was your interaction with this person?
- Did they seem attractive to you?
- Were you able to establish a rapport or connection with them?
- Were you able to let them into your space?
- Did you feel included in their world?
- Was it a joyful interaction for you?

I think I can safely assume you said NO to all of the above. Because that's the truth. When someone is being fake and pretending to be who they are not, one cannot establish a relationship or a rapport with them because they are standing behind a facade. It's nothing but a barrier which prevents gifting and receiving between the two of them. It also makes them unattractive.

I've noticed a few people do this when they are performing on stage or presenting in front of an audience. I have been there, done that, too. I have tried to be someone whom the audience will like, losing my originality in the process. Even though our audience may not notice this cognitively, they get it energetically, like we do, most of the time. People fail to build a rapport and establish connection with their audience, who in turn lose interest in listening to what you have to say or offer. On the contrary, I have seen famous celebrities who are very vulnerable and authentic whether in person or on stage. Have you wondered what makes them attractive? It's not just their looks, it's who they be, and it's their vulnerability!

Being vulnerable makes you extremely attractive, irresistible and beautiful! When people see you they say to themselves "I want to have what this person is having!" People don't even know what it is about you that they are so attracted to, but they are! When you are vulnerable you include people in your world; they feel closer to you; and there is a beautiful intimacy that gets created, because they have access to the real you. That's the beauty of it. It reminds me of Brene Brown's quote *"What makes you vulnerable, makes you beautiful."*

It is not about the physical looks, it is who you are from within that people are attracted to. You have to be willing for your real self to step out and show up in front of people. You have to be willing to show yourself completely and utterly without holding back for the fear of rejection or judgment. Yes, I expose my true self and I have no filters. So what if I

41

am wrong? So what if I come across as weird or stupid? No one is right or perfect. These are just rose-colored lenses through which we view the world and these lenses can keep changing. They are all forms of judgments.

Judgment is a huge turn-off. If you have been around someone who judges themselves a lot, has extremely low self-esteem and hate themselves, do they seem attractive? Not really. If you judge yourself, you are not being vulnerable because judgment is also a barrier. The purpose of judment is to create separation. In this case, it is separating you from you. When you have judgments of you, people sense that energetically – even if they don't cognitively see it and they don't want to be around you. Choosing to let go of my self-judgments was a huge part of me choosing to be more vulnerable.

"Your real, genuine self is the most attractive aspect of YOU."

I didn't discover all this overnight. I learnt it over time. When I started to facilitate classes, I tried to be the "best facilitator" and teach my classes the same way as other facilitators whom I admire. I failed at it miserably because I was trying to be someone else. When I chose to be authentic while I facilitated classes, it was more fun for me, and way easier than before. I was willing to fail, make mistakes, laugh it out, tell people "I don't know" when they asked me a question and I didn't have any information to give them.

I did this without judging myself as small and less. I was comfortable being raw, open and transparent and showing myself completely to my participants, without holding back for the fear of being judged as a 'bad facilitator'.

I was also open to talk about my life, my very personal stories, and experiences in classes. I was able to shift and change things for me, without worrying about what opinions that would create in people. It was incredible to see that people got more change out of my classes than before, when I chose to be that vulnerable. They said they got inspired listening to my stories and that the space of 'no judgment' I had created gave them the space to shift and change dynamically. I was gob-smacked!

I've had multiple instances where my clients have told me they saw my photo on the website and there was something about me they found attractive, so they chose to come to my classes or see me for a session. Looks like the lack of judgment was showing up on my face too! We all have the capacity to pick up a zillion things energetically than we give ourselves credit for! I did not realize the gift and power of vulnerability until I started choosing it and being it in my life and received feedback from people around me as to what it created for them.

When I was choosing to be more authentic and real, little did I know this is what would get created. Heck, I didn't even know I was being vulnerable until people came up to me and said all this! I had assumed vulnerability would show up in a very different way and I wasn't even aware that I was being it. At times I have judged myself too, for not being it. It is insane how much we love judgments.

While I was navigating through this insanity, I had a chat with Dain Heer and he said,

> *"You can't see what you be. You can only be what you be. You can be aware of what you be, but not cognitively understand it most of the times. It is only when someone goes to describe you from the outside and put these characteristics into words that you look at it and become aware of what you are being. It doesn't look or feel the way you think it is going to. Ever. Even when you are in the middle of choosing what you are asking for, you will not feel like you are choosing what you are asking for, because you think you will feel a certain way when you are choosing it and if it doesn't show up that way you will not even receive it."*

I can't thank him enough for this conversation, as it was a total game-changer for me. This was the moment I stopped judging and started receiving everything that I was already being. I stopped looking for it outside of me and started acknowledging how much I am already being it and also asked for more of it to show up.

What if you do not judge and have no expectation of what being vulnerable will look like? All you have to do is keep choosing it every moment. Can you be open to receiving whatever it creates in your life, no matter how that looks like or feels like? More magic gets created when you have zero expectations or fixed points of views. Expectations are also barriers that we create to block the magic from coming into our lives.

My journey of choosing to be more vulnerable has been one of the most fulfilling and exciting journeys I've ever chosen in my life so far. It has opened up those hidden parts of me – who I truly am – that wasn't available to me prior to making this choice of finding who I really am. I had no idea that I had even embarked on a journey and one day it would lead me here, sharing my experiences with you through this book. When I started, I was at a place where I was extremely sceptical, whether I had any gifts or greatness in me to find?! But I was still willing to choose it, be in the question and explore. I now recognize the power of choice and what it can create. The more you choose for you, choose to unleash all aspects of you, you will see that the universe has your back all the time. You will also find more people who are willing to have your back.

I personally don't like to wait much for anything and I'd love to have everything NOW! But one thing I do know is that vulnerability may not come overnight. I stopped judging myself for not having it all immediately. Honestly, it is a muscle that one has to build. It comes with practice. You also have to choose it. Choice triumphs everything else. You make a demand of yourself to choose it. What does that look like, you wonder? It is like stomping your foot and saying "This has to change right now and I am willing to do whatever it takes to change it!" This demand ignites the spark and creates an energy and space that will attract more of what you are asking for into your life. I wish to emphasize again that you have to first make the choice. Choice always has to come first. Everything else will follow. When you begin to practice it and continue to choose it every moment, it'll become easy and effortless. It becomes a part of your lifestyle and a way of being.

I am extremely grateful for every single person who has inspired me and had my back on this journey. I also don't forget that finally it is me who is choosing all of it and taking action. So I remember to acknowledge me and be grateful for ME, for having made these life-changing, reality-changing choices that have given me more access to myself than I never knew existed before.

I am becoming someone that I never imagined was possible. I am also now willing to have my own back and I am grateful to me for that too! With this gratitude comes the acknowledgement of how much change I am choosing in this one lifetime that I have (though it seems like I've had a hundred lifetimes in this one life), and keeps me moving forward to choose more and more of it. Every time I make a life transforming choice (several of them mentioned in this book), I say "Wow, that was amazing, is there something more beyond this? And the universe says – yes and presents me another possibility. I choose that and my life grows by leaps and bounds!"

Chapter 3

Embracing Courage and Strength

While I was digging deeper to know what being vulnerable is, I came across **Brené Brown's** Ted Talk on the power of vulnerability and went on to read her book *"Daring Greatly"*. It gave me a very different perspective on this topic and I absolutely adore her and her work. I started to see how vulnerability is the source of courage, strength and potency. (Potency is the ability to change anything). It's the courage to be you, to be real and authentic, to be out there naked in the world with total transparency and in complete allowance of your imperfections. It allows you to be who you are without any frills attached, nothing to cover up your limitations.

When I look at the past, I find it crazy that most of my choices used to be influenced by what other people thought about me. I had to gather a lot of courage to be my authentic self as I let go of other people's opinions about me, even if they thought I am weird and strange. I am fine with that as I no longer see my weirdness as a wrongness! It is my way of being different. Having courage and cultivating authenticity have been the true gifts and power of vulnerability for me.

To be fair, I have to give myself some credit for having the courage to do a lot of things differently in my life – not conforming to the culture and traditions of being an Indian and an 'Indian woman' more specifically. I got married when I was 28, and to the man of my choice. It is unacceptable in my culture and community for women to get married so late and not have an arranged marriage. I still waited, without giving in to the family or societal pressure, because I wanted to choose when I was ready and when I knew it was the right time for me. I had a couple of relationships with men before I got married – which is again unacceptable in my culture. I had never travelled out of India, but I chose to fly all alone to a new country to meet a man (who is now my husband). He was a stranger at that point, as we had not seen each other before, only spoken over the phone for a month!

I earned a Master's degree in Business Administration, was working in a multi-national company, earning a hefty pay package, having fun, being independent and living life on my own terms. This was not typical of a middle class Indian woman in my community, who is the only daughter to her parents.

When it came to having the courage to choose me, stand up for me, speak my truth and honor me, I definitely didn't do a good job. I sucked at it. I would agree with somebody simply because I hated being confrontational and having a different point of view (gosh!). I would give up me at the drop of a hat and be miserable for days. I was great at it. To a certain extent I loved playing a victim, so I didn't have to be the one responsible for my life. When I gave that up and claimed, owned and acknowledged that I am the one solely responsible for everything that is created in my life, things started to change and my life has been changing so dynamically in the past couple of years that I have no sense of who I was even a month ago!

I just kept choosing, choosing and choosing, keeping "me" in focus, every moment of my life. When it was not obvious to me that I was embracing courage during this process, Dain Heer pointed it out to me during a session, as to how I've had a lot of courage and the willingness to let my entire life change and be greater. He mentioned my courage in various other occasions and there was no way I could NOT see it within me anymore. Very few people in this world have this gift of seeing the greatness that you are choosing, and when they acknowledge you for choosing that, it changes your life. So when I say Dain Heer has been a huge gift in my life, this is a part of the gift that he is. I wouldn't be writing about courage here if not for him bringing it to my awareness that I have a lot of it.

I am someone who gets the energy of things easily, long before I understand it cognitively. When I am being something, I have no idea that I am being it, unless someone outside of me sees it and brings it to my awareness. That's when I absorb it, recognize it, let it sink in, receive more of it and ponder it to understand at a cognitive level so that I am able to describe it in words here. In fact this entire book on vulnerability wouldn't have been written if not for the gift and contribution that Dain Heer has been for me, and that's not an exaggeration!

The most important aspect of any transformational

journey is to recognize where you already ARE being what you are asking for, to a certain extent, and also acknowledge yourself for choosing more change as you go through the journey. The more you recognize you are choosing it and give yourself the credit for it, the easier your journey gets.

"Where in your life are you already being vulnerable and courageous that you if you did acknowledge it, would allow more of it to show up?"

Once I recognized and accepted that I am someone who has a lot of courage, I spent hours contemplating – what does courage mean to me? Thanks to this book, I would have otherwise never thought of or attempted to describe that in words! I've given it my best shot here.

> *"To me, courage is about following my dreams, getting my desires into action, embracing my awareness and knowing, trusting myself unconditionally – even if no one else in the world trusts me. It's seeking endless possibilities, plenty of which exist out there in the universe untapped and unknown. It is a willingness to take the risk of bringing my ideas into fruition in my own unique way and make big choices that have the potency to change the world."*

There you go! I think I did a pretty good job at describing that. Ha Ha!

When I say it is the willingness to take the risk of bringing my ideas into fruition in my own unique way, what comes to mind is my choice of writing this book on this topic. Even though vulnerability is not a common topic, there are still people who have already written great books on it, one of them being Brené Brown. As I started writing this, I had lot of judgments come up like – why would anyone want to read another book on vulnerability when there are a few good ones already out there? I am not an expert on this topic, according to this reality because I am not a scientist who has done extensive research, or given a Ted Talk or have any credentials that are noteworthy. Based on this, I did put aside the book for a few weeks and decided not to go ahead with it.

While I pondered about courage, it dawned upon me that I am an expert on this topic of vulnerability in my own way. The way I can talk about vulnerability, no one else can. I've had the courage to be authentic, real and different in my life in several ways. My experiences, my story of how I embraced it, the kind of life I had before and the way I have chosen to transform it using various tools and techniques, the people who have influenced and inspired me in this journey and my learnings in the process, the words I use, the instances I quote are very unique to me. That's the difference that each one of us is. Who you be, the qualities and characteristics that you possess and the gift that you are, makes your product unique, even if something similar already exists. All of this is greater than any credentials this reality can use in order to validate and define you. This is a part of having the courage to be you. People who are masters of courage, are the ones who have embodied vulnerability in their being. They have opened themselves up completely to whatever comes their way that they are not aware of. Good and Bad, both.

It's crazy to see how we stop ourselves from showing up in this world with our brilliance. I noticed I was the one stopping me, no one else. I had to get out of my own way. Have you ever been apologetic when you have shared your ideas or creations in this world? I have, several times before. When I wrote on my blog , or posted a video of mine on social media or shared some other piece of creative work, I would do it from the space of – *I am sorry if this is not good, I've never shared this before, please don't judge me, hope you like it*. I was making myself less and small.

When you operate from this space of "I am not good enough" people can sense that and they see your work with those lenses of judgments. When I chose courage, acknowledged my brilliance of creating something and then shared my ideas out in the world, I was inviting people to a different possibility, to acknowledge their own brilliance, talents and capacities.

"Who would you be and what would you choose today if you had the courage to embrace your difference right away?"

Sometimes all you require is a starting point. The moment I recognized that I do have a lot of courage, it was like going on a treasure hunt inside me to find all those unacknowledged areas of my greatness and strength. I could see all those places where I have been courageous and continue to choose it. Even as I write this book, I choose courage as I am aware that what I write will be read by hundreds or thousands of people. A friend of mine recently pointed out something about the way I dress, how I dress different now than I did previously. When I heard that, I went, oh yes, she is indeed correct! This change has been so subtle that I failed to notice it.

As I've mentioned earlier, hiding myself, making me small and insignificant used to be my safe cocoon. So my dressing style and the way I used to be with my body portrayed exactly that. I didn't want to look too nice, sexy or beautiful because then I would be seen! I cut off my sensuality so that I don't attract attention from people and I could be quiet and hidden when I wanted to. And then I would also wonder why nobody noticed me and gave me attention and made myself miserable for that! That's what I call insanity! How many of you do that with your bodies to ensure it matches the beliefs you hold? Our bodies do exactly what we ask it to do and be. It complies with the judgments we hold and shows up exactly matching that.

As I became more comfortable in my own skin, dissolved my boundaries, and had the courage to embrace my sexualness, my body automatically started to look different and it picked clothes that made it look sexy, ravishing and stunning. Today I can walk through a room full of people and be at total ease with everyone looking at me. I can receive compliments about my body and the way I look, very comfortably too. Recently in a class, I had at least 20 people walk up to me and say "*You look beautiful and sexy*". This wasn't part of my reality a year ago, for sure. This was not something I expected to show up either but hey, **change never shows up the way you think it will!** These golden words said by Dain Heer are something I always remember, maybe you should highlight them too! As you explore this topic and make different choices, your life will change in ways you never expected it to and these words will be a saviour then.

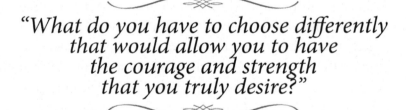

"What do you have to choose differently that would allow you to have the courage and strength that you truly desire?"

There are several other areas where I've been able to choose vulnerability and the courage to be different. These are some of the things that most of us don't even notice or give importance to. That's exactly why I list them here. These may be areas where you are already choosing to be courageous or it might inspire you to choose it as you read along:

- courage to travel alone, visit another corner of the world just to see what I can create because it is fun for me

- courage to be the kindness I truly am and not toning it down because other people cannot receive it

- courage to receive judgments about me, my choices, my creations and everything else

- courage to let go of everyone and everything. When you are not willing to let go of someone or something, that person or thing controls you and holds you back

- courage to create my life the way I desire – not the way I was told it should be like

- courage to dream big and actualize those dreams into reality

- courage to nurture my ideas into fruition without judging if they are good enough

- courage to choose for "me", make "me" the most valuable person and never make myself small and anyone else greater than me

- courage to get out of my comfort zone, no matter how cozy it is to be there and how hard it is to get out of it

- courage to choose an adventurous living. I am extremely grateful for my husband for showing me what it is like to live an adventurous life!

- courage to acknowledge that I am a gift, a contribution to people around and I am changing the world, in my own way!

> ## "What is that one thing you can do different today that will lead you towards creating the life you desire?"

If you are avoiding vulnerability, you are not taking risks. You are not choosing courage. You are denying who you really are. I am sure most of you will agree with me that courage would not be possible if I was being fake, trying to hide my flaws, lived in a box or have barriers around me. It does require authenticity. I cannot emphasize that enough. It requires embracing the real you, knowing your strengths and acknowledging that you are a gift to this planet. This is a space where other people's judgments of you no longer bother you. (Trust me, it is a lot of time and energy wasted if you care about what this society or other people think about you!) You stop caring about what people think and start creating your life and doing what is fun for you. That is true gift of vulnerability! It opens up a great amount of power and potential in you and your life. Instead of feeling weak, you feel powerful and strong.

Chapter 4

Going Beyond Comfort Zone

Being vulnerable is about getting out of the safety of your comfort zone and venturing out into the unknown and trusting yourself completely throughout the journey. This is something I have explored extensively and chosen every moment of my life for the past few years.

Stepping out of comfort zone would mean different things for different people, and each person's experience is different and unique. For me personally, traveling the world has been one of the most rewarding experiences that showed me what it truly means to go beyond my zone of comfort. In the chapter on courage, I mentioned that traveling was one of the things in my life that opened up a lot of courage and vulnerability for me. Especially traveling alone.

I always wanted to travel the world and explore new places. But I lived a very protective life for 28 years, courtesy of my parents. Whether they were over-protective because I was their only child or it was their own insecurities, I have no idea and it doesn't matter. The fact is I was never allowed to venture out of the house on my own in the same city until

I was accepted into the university. Even when I started working in the corporate world, I was constantly supervised. It was a great deal of effort to convince them when I wanted to go on a vacation with my friends. So my travels were limited to only road trips to nearby cities around Bangalore, south of India, where I lived.

In short, this is the background I came from, but I knew the world is my oyster and I was eager to explore it. I was asking the universe what would it take for that to show up and I ended up marrying my husband who loves to travel and have an adventurous living! Love is an understatement to express his passion for traveling and I love the fact that we share that passion and joy for it. That's how I started to travel the world, with him. In the five years we have been married to each other, we have visited at least 90+ cities all over the world together and it's been an extraordinary adventure.

Traveling with my husband was easy because I knew I had someone to depend on. The challenging part was when I had to travel alone as part of my business, to facilitate workshops and classes. Traveling alone is not something I had planned for when I started my business. It was not doing very well in Singapore because the people were not yet open to these kind of classes. The energies from other places were calling me. I was at a point where I could choose courage, jump off the cliff and live my dream life that I always wanted to have or choose to live in the confines of my boundaries and the safe cocoon I had created so that nothing changes. Obviously I chose the former.

Flying into a new country all by myself, staying alone in

a hotel room, finding my way around there, eating out alone, hanging out with strangers – just the thought of these things would get me petrified and I was scared to death. Do you notice that the 'fear' aspect comes up a lot when you choose to be vulnerable? We use fear as an excuse to not choose greater things in life. I had briefly mentioned at the beginning of this book that fear is not real, it is a lie, a construct. We are the ones who give it significance and make it real and true. When I heard Gary Douglas say that fear and excitement feel exactly the same, I did not understand it for a long time.

When I travelled alone for the first time and I thought I was scared, I asked, "Is this fear or excitement I am sensing?" It was actually the excitement of doing something new, choosing to accomplish my dreams, finally doing things I always wanted to do for three decades of my life. This clearly wasn't fear. We always misidentify excitement to be fear. Next time try asking this question. If you don't get it the first time, don't give up. It took me months before I could actually understand this and see it work! So when I stopped calling what I was sensing as 'fear' and instead told myself I am 'excited', everything started getting lighter. Now I was excited to embark on an adventurous journey that would take me closer to where I wanted to go and what I wanted to create.

Another thing about fear is it may not be yours. You might have heard stories from other people about their similar experiences, or read it in books or watched in movies and you buy into their point of view, as if they knew better than you did. So another great question to ask, "Is this fear mine or is it a point of view I bought from someone or somewhere else?"

"What if fear is not real?
Is it even yours or are you buying into
someone else's concept of fear?
Is it fear or excitement?"

I went beyond fear, but I was still not comfortable. To say that I was extremely uncomfortable choosing this would be an understatement. I was like a fish out of water, not knowing if I would survive it all. But I knew it was my choice. I was not doing this out of a necessity or because someone had asked me to do this. Facilitating classes, meeting new people, seeing their lives change in front of my eyes gives me immense joy and pleasure. When I am facilitating, I am truly being me.

So I'll do whatever it takes to have more of facilitating every day, every moment of my life. But the discomfort was very real too. I couldn't ignore that. I was judging it as wrong and that I shouldn't be feeling uncomfortable. Why? Because I always thought being comfortable is being normal, or else there was something wrong. I have no idea where I bought this point of view from, but I remember when I was a kid and I was uncomfortable, my parents would ask me what's wrong? As I grew up, other people around me would ask the same question.

So somewhere, somehow I had concluded that discomfort is negative and bad. When I let go of this judgment, I no longer had to work towards getting rid of the discomfort. I asked myself, "What would it take to enjoy this discomfort and have fun with it?" That question shifted everything and made things very easy. This is a question I still use very often. It's been a few years but there are times I still feel uncomfortable when I visit new countries or I have to do something that I've never done before. I now enjoy the discomfort and interestingly, it has ALWAYS opened up more doorways and possibilities for me, given me access to more of "me" and my talents and capacities. So I actually love choosing things that make me uncomfortable because I know it creates something greater, way beyond my imagination.

"What if discomfort is normal? What if you chose five different things this week/month/year that make you uncomfortable and take you out of your comfort zone and see what that creates?"

Not trusting me was one of the biggest safety cocoons I had built for me. Whenever something came up for me or I had to make a choice, it was most comfortable and easy to say "I don't know" to myself. That response came in a jiffy, even before I could think. That was my way of denying my knowing. And then I'd seek answers or awareness from somebody else and even if what they said felt heavy and untrue, there are times I have followed it and it has created crap in my life. I'd do this because I was not ready to be responsible for my choices. Those few times where I've pushed myself out of this comfort zone, trusted my knowing and made choices – like getting married to my husband, changing my profession, quitting my job and starting my own business, these are the times when I've had major breakthroughs. Those choices completely transformed my life and put me on a path where I wanted the journey to go. It wasn't easy for me to get out of this comfort zone of not trusting me. To be honest it was one of the toughest things I had to learn to do, for myself. But every time I chose it and I saw how it changed my life and what it created and generated for me, I wanted to have more of that! So what if "easy" is not what determines what you choose or don't choose? You simply choose it, look at what it creates for you and see if you wish to have a lot more of that in and as your life?

By making yourself vulnerable, you give yourself the leeway to step outside and go out of the safety net that you've built. With my experience described above, you will notice that it is mostly about our mindset and way of thinking. We are more conditioned to look at the wrongness of things than to ask "What is right about this that I am not acknowledging?" (Another powerful tool of Access Consciousness® that I love!)

When I stepped outside of my zone of comfort, what came out of it was my willingness to fail, willingness to be disliked by people, and the willingness to tread on an unknown path. None of which I was willing to have or be in my life previously. So I would be fine with doing the same thing in life over and over, making the same choices and keep expecting a different result to show up. I am sure a few of you would resonate with this absurdity. The reality is, you will never know until you try it. As Gary Douglas says over and over again, "*Choice always creates awareness*". You choose something, you get an awareness whether it works for you or not. Then you can choose something different. It is all about choice, choice and more choice! If you are not choosing, you are probably getting into your comfort zone. To stay there is also a choice. There is no right or wrong about it. It's all about whether it is working for you or not. Would you like something different, or not?

"What if behind every resistance lies a capacity?"

I have talked about how fear is not real, yet we use fear to limit ourselves. I lived three decades of my life with lots of fears and let it control me. I felt like I cut off parts of me to live a life based on fear. When I learned the tools of Access Consciousness®, this started to change. I realized what I was feeling most of the times was excitement which I used to label as fear. It is interesting that I married a man who is completely opposite of me. My husband doesn't know what fear is and he loves adventure, extreme sports and anything that gets him to push his limits. He inspired me to a large extent to let go of my fears and go beyond my limitations.

We were in Queenstown, the adventure capital of

New Zealand a few years back and my husband, being an adrenaline junkie, had signed up for various extreme sports activities. Just looking at those would bring up huge walls of resistance in me. But I knew I wanted to get out of my comfort zone and go beyond the "fear" aspect. After much hesitation I was ready to do my first tandem skydive from 12,000 ft. It was one of the most exhilarating and rewarding experiences of my life. A lot of crazy, weird stuff came up for me as I sat in the plane. I used every tool and technique that I knew during the flight, it made me feel slightly better. I was still extremely petrified and soon realized it was not fear but actually excitement. So after 15 minutes, in those final moments before jumping out of the plane, I had to choose– I could either make this the worst experience of my life or the best experience. I said 'Fuck It' and took the plunge, trusting the universe and choosing to receive the experience in totality and have fun. It felt immensely rewarding and was one of the best learning experiences of my life. It showed me the power of choice.

With every situation, the way we choose to receive that experience is what makes it different. All it takes is few seconds to choose. You can contemplate on changing something or doing something for days, weeks or months and yet not change. When you make the choice, things can change in matter of seconds. At some point in life, you just need to take the leap. That takes courage and vulnerability. When I made the choice and took the plunge from the plane, I didn't know then, but I know now that I was being very vulnerable – I was embracing courage, willing to take the risk, being present in the moment, lowering my barriers to receive the experience with ease, trusting myself and the universe, and breaking out of my shell. All it took was a choice.

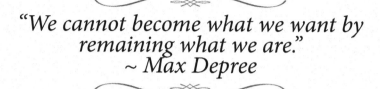

> *"We cannot become what we want by remaining what we are."*
> *~ Max Depree*

There are many ways you can be vulnerable – initiating conversation with a stranger, quitting a job that you hate, starting a new business, getting into a relationship, and so forth. Choosing adventure and extreme sports was one of the ways for me to be vulnerable, other than traveling alone. If you don't get out of your safe place, you may remain the same person or have the same kind of life, tomorrow, the next day and the next!

Vulnerability creates a platform for personal growth. Some of my old friends refuse to get out of their status quo or bring changes into their lives. They are content with the comfort they have created and their lives are largely the same way it used to be when I met them several years back. They are fine with it. I am no one to judge. It's not a wrongness to maintain your status quo. It is only a choice. I did that for several years too. After a certain point it didn't work for me. So I chose something different. Stepping out of my comfort zone allowed me to expand the zone in which I create and operate.

Every time I expand that zone, I have access to several

new possibilities which wouldn't show up otherwise. I unlocked my gifts and abilities that I didn't have access to before, then my field of awareness expands as well and I am now having fewer limitations! I am never the same person I was, with every choice I make. So my question to you (if you are not already choosing it) is this: You would not choose this for what reason? Maybe it is something to ponder?

"You cannot expect to create a different result by making the same old choices. If you wish to create a different outcome, make a different choice."

Letting go of my comfort zone has been a huge learning for me in the past year specifically. The biggest comfort zone I had was of "no change". I lived in a conflictual state where I desired things to change in my life but I equally resisted change as well. Last year I made a demand of myself to step out of my comfort zone in every single solitary choice I make, in every area of my life.

There are times when I have felt like I am falling apart during this process. Hanging in there and having the courage to go through it has created much more ease, joy and possibilities, every single time! It feels like courage and comfort are mutually exclusive. You cannot have both at the same time. Now I have started to enjoy the discomfort because I know that there is a dynamic transformation at the end of it and I get to access more of ME each time I step out of it. Every time I have chosen something that is beyond my perceived comfort zone, it has truly expanded my life exponentially. I've heard Gary Douglas say *"Discomfort is ten seconds before you have all of YOU."* True that is!

So everywhere you have created your 'safe comfort zone' as your necessity are you willing to give that up and let it go? What if stepping out and choosing beyond your zone of comfort is what is required for you to create an extraordinary life with unlimited possibilities?

"How different would you and your life be if you chose today to break out of the irresistible spell of living in your comfort zone, forever?"

One courageous thing I still keep choosing every day is to never go back to living in my safety cocoon in any area of my life, ever again, no matter what, no matter how uncomfortable it feels. I love the difference that it creates for me and the clarity and fun it brings to my world.

Chapter 5

Building Trust

I have been able to create a beautiful life that works for me through the process of trusting me. Doubting myself was a familiar territory, and served as my comfort zone for most of my life. I was always looking to 'fit in' which obviously meant I didn't trust myself enough. My inner critic was much louder compared to my feeble voice of trust. The former one always took over. One way I have explored trust is by exploring vulnerability. It took me time to know that vulnerability and trust go hand in hand. To be vulnerable requires a great deal of trusting yourself and in order to trust yourself completely, you must be willing to be vulnerable. To expose your strengths and flaws, to be comfortable receiving judgments and/or compliments – all of which require a certain degree of security and inner strength which comes from trusting yourself.

Can you open up to someone you don't trust? No. Clearly, then it is not possible to open up to you, if you don't trust YOU. Distrust is a huge barrier that separates you from you.

In my opinion, it is one of the most unkind things you can do to yourself. Of course, we cannot trust ourselves if we don't love and honor ourselves either. When we love ourselves we are able to rely on our instincts/knowing/awareness and be vulnerable to them.

When you trust yourself, making choices become easy and effortless. You may choose something unconventional and strange which doesn't make any logical sense. If you trust you and the universe, and be vulnerable to receive what's been offered to you, it will surely lead you to a place that is far greater than you could ever imagine. You let go of control and allow yourself to receive the contribution from the universe and you.

Have you ever trusted someone in your life and then went on to see how mean or vicious they got? Perhaps they backstabbed you or you realized they didn't have your back, they were just pretending? I did, a few times. So I asked myself – was that really trust I had or was it blind faith? It was the latter. Trust is not blind faith, that's the lie we buy into. It is your willingness to be present without your guard up and be aware of the truth whether it is good, bad or ugly. See people for who they are, see the reality of the situation rather than going into assumptions or conclusions. So when I realized this, I also recognized that the very first time I met these few people in my life, I already had an awareness of them, that they were mean, vicious or pretentious. I shut this awareness off, thinking that I was judging them. I created a huge wall of doubt about my own awareness, until the time I was hit by a hammer so that I couldn't NOT see the truth anymore. I am sure you can relate to this too, from a similar instance in your own life.

Right now, take a situation where you feel stuck in your life and you feel you don't have any clarity and you are looking for a solution on what's the best thing to do. It could be something in a relationship that is not working, or a job, or with money or business. Now take a moment, lower all your barriers you have with this situation/people involved. Receive all the awareness 100 percent without filtering it or doubting any of it, no matter how irrational, illogical, impractical or unrealistic it may feel. Now just look at it with no point of view – were you already aware that this would not work out, in the very beginning, even before you started it? That would be a Yes. Acknowledge the subtle feather touch of awareness that you had at the very beginning. So the truth is, we all are aware, every moment, in every choice we make. But the reality is we don't trust that awareness and follow our knowing with every choice we make. Everywhere things are going great in your life is when you are trusting your knowing completely, and anywhere things are not working out for you is when you are going against your knowing. It is as simple as that!

Imagine what would your life be like if you trusted your awareness with every choice you make? And you didn't need somebody else's approval whether the choice you are making is right or wrong or good or bad. Because what they tell you is through their own judgments and it's their awareness, not yours. You and only YOU know what is true for you. No one else does. So anytime you are looking for answers, approval or validation from somebody else (teachers, gurus, parents, bosses, friends, etc.) about what you know, you are invalidating yourself and your own awareness. That keeps separating you from you and doesn't take you any closer to creating an intimate relationship with you. It's about being the 'guru' of your own life. That doesn't mean I don't discuss things with people or ask them for suggestions. I do. But at the end, I always follow what I know is true. When somebody tells me something, I ask a question, is this true for me? I don't blindly buy into what they say.

Now, that being said, I don't share everything I know, every awareness I have, with others. I'd definitely not recommend that to you either. There are several times when I have shared my ideas or awareness with somebody and they just shot it down, thought I was crazy, laughed at it or said that's not true. It created a doubt in myself. The truth is, they were not yet willing to receive that information. So it is not required that you share everything that you know with people around you. That includes your spouses, your significant other and all your near and dear ones. Always ask – what information is this person willing to receive, and tell them exactly that much. Just because I meet somebody, even if that's a client and I get an awareness of what's going on in their life, doesn't mean I share it with them. You have to let people get to their own awareness of things. You telling them will not make them accept it any better.

Learning to keep my mouth shut about what I know is one of the smartest things I've learnt to do. I don't stick my foot in my mouth anymore nor do I have to invalidate my own knowing. It has made my life easy peasy! I invite you to try it too, and see what that creates for you!

"What would your life be like if you trusted YOU and your awareness 1000 percent, ALL of the time?"

As I mentioned in the very beginning of this book, I was always looking for others to give me the "right answers" as if they knew about me better than I did. Building trust is about asking questions and getting to your own awareness of what is true for you and what isn't. I am extremely grateful for the tools of Access Consciousness®. These tools played a key role in empowering me to trust myself. I stopped seeking other people to make choices for me or to determine what's a right choice or a wrong choice.

It's taken me a lot of courage and being vulnerable to reach this point where I am now willing to trust me, even if no one else does. Even if the entire world says something opposite of what I know! This reminds me of an instance in my life six years ago which is a great example of this. I had just started talking to this guy over the phone (who is now my husband). He lived in Dubai and was introduced to me by my parents, over an email. All I had seen was his photographs on social media. We instantly clicked and spoke for hours for a month. I knew that there was a greater possibility here for us. My awareness was stronger than ever before. I decided to travel to Dubai to meet and get to know him better. It was my first time travelling out of India and to meet a stranger. It didn't feel weird at all in my world like it did for my friends and family, who thought I was crazy to do this. I was told repeatedly of all the things that could go wrong and why I shouldn't take a risk. There were times when I almost bought into their points of view and was willing to give it up. I am glad I didn't. I made my awareness more valuable and didn't make my family or friends greater than me.

Six years ago I didn't have any of the tools and techniques I have now. I didn't know what it meant to follow energy, but I can see now, I was doing exactly that! I was listening to the whispers of the future and sensing the possibility of a nurturing, expansive and phenomenal relationship between me and him. I am very grateful that I trusted myself 1000 percent to make that choice. To say that one choice changed my entire life is an understatement. I've been married to the same guy for five years now and the energy of a phenomenal relationship that I was aware of then is what is present in our lives right now and it keeps getting better and better every day.

What similar choices do you have available for you right now, waiting to be chosen, that you have not yet chosen, and if you would choose, it would shift gears and change your life beyond what you can fathom?

"Do you trust YOU or your judgments?"

When you trust you and the universe, you have no resistance to receiving any kind of information that the universe has to offer to you – the good, bad or ugly from the past, present or future. Being vulnerable opens up a space for you to receive wisps of awareness from the future. This is very subtle, like a soft gentle feather touch. If you trust it, you can receive it completely, or else it goes unnoticed. A couple of times when my husband and I were planning our vacations, certain dates felt very strange and heavy. Even though it made logical sense to choose it, I have trusted those wisps of awareness and changed the itinerary. It's only later we saw there were earthquakes both times in those countries after we left. Had I not trusted my awareness and changed the dates, we would have been present during the disasters. There are several other occasions where something similar to this has shown up during our travels and I was willing to trust my knowing. I now trust my awareness more strongly than ever before, every single time I plan our itinerary or book a hotel.

When it comes to my business, sometimes I plan to attend a class in another corner of the world, more than a year in advance because the energy is pulling me there very strongly. There are times when I travel 20+ hours to attend a class for just three days when I could have attended it online anyways. It doesn't look practical and sounds crazy in my head but energetically it feels light. These are the classes where I have received maximum change and they have been catalysts to transforming my life exponentially. I am so grateful to myself for trusting my knowing and choosing to be present there. I always am amazed seeing that the universe has my back, every single time. I have learnt to trust it. I haven't been that smart always. I have ignored this awareness several times and felt miserable.

There are times when a friend wanted to meet for dinner, or an appointment for a client had already been given, or I had committed to attend a party and the awareness says don't do it, but because of my own stupid reasons I still went ahead with it and later felt pathetic, lousy and miserable or my body felt sick. Then I've wondered why the hell did I not trust my awareness? I knew this would happen in the first place! That's called getting hit by a hammer when you don't listen to the feather touch of awareness. I have made some crazy choices in my life when I haven't trusted me and every one of those choices created a lot of crap! Have you ever taken a job that you hated or said yes to a relationship which made you miserable? That you knew well in advance these wouldn't work out, even before you started it, but still you went ahead? That's what I am talking about! Been there, done that. We all learn from our choices and experiences, don't we?

Five years ago in 2010, I made a choice trusting my knowing, based only on the wisps of awareness I received. I quit my corporate job because I was getting married and moving to Dubai to live with my husband. I had planned to take a break before I resumed work. Those few months that I took off were extremely beautiful and joyful. I had forgotten to appreciate life, and notice and be grateful to all the small things that bring pleasure and joy. I had not taken time out to nurture me among the busy deadlines, projects and meetings. I always knew I didn't enjoy the work I was doing and wanted something different where I could be more of ME and use my talents and capacities. I didn't know to what extent I disliked my job until I took this break. I spent time learning things that were fun for me. I got a certification as a Clinical Hypnotherapist and a life coach and also learnt various healing modalities like Reiki, Pranic Healing, EFT (Emotional Freedom Technique), NLP (Neuro Linguistic Programming) and more. I knew this was where my capacity and interest lies, in facilitating people and transforming lives and I wanted to do this full time. Just the thought of making this transition expanded my world and made me extremely happy. That is a wisp of awareness from the future, and I was willing to receive. I knew I didn't want to go back to the corporate world to do what I was doing.

If you thought jumping out of a plane requires a lot of courage, I'd say it took me ten times more courage and vulnerability to trust myself and my awareness, and quit my well-paying job to start a new business of my own. I was aware I was giving up a lot of benefits, financial security and stability in my life when I made this choice and I was jumping into the unknown, with a leap of faith. It wasn't easy and it was extremely uncomfortable to take the plunge. Deep down in my heart I knew this is what I wanted to do so I was willing to take the risk. I did not want to be stuck in a job I hated and feel like a lion trapped in a cage. I had no idea how this would work out, what it would look like, how I would create it – absolutely nothing. We had moved to Singapore by then, which was a new territory for me, and I didn't know a single soul here. So it looked all the more daunting. I was terrified to say the least. (I didn't know back then that it was excitement I was feeling and not fear. I didn't have these tools!) Many people told me I was crazy to make this drastic transition, especially after getting a masters degree in Business from one of the top 20 business schools in the world and having a successful career.

I knew I was not existing. I wasn't thriving. I wasn't happy. So I was willing to trust me and my knowing, no matter who said what. My point of view was that I would rather have less money and be joyful doing what I enjoy than have loads of money and be miserable. I am grateful for myself that I trusted my 'knowing' and that's what gave me the courage and strength to be vulnerable to make this life changing choice. I have reached a place in my life now when I have to make a choice and even if one single molecule or fibre in my body is screaming "NO! That doesn't work!" I trust it. Because I know what happens when I go against my knowing and I am not choosing to create that as my life anymore.

> *"How different would you and your life be if you trusted every single awareness you have?"*

More often than not, your awareness of the future does not make logical sense or sound practical because your 'knowing' goes beyond your five senses, beyond what your mind can even fathom. It is a realm where mind does not exist. So if you are using your mind to make sense out of the awareness you get, you are limiting yourself and diminishing your awareness, A LOT! If our logical mind could figure everything out, don't you think we would have figured it all out long ago?

One of my favorite tools of Access Consciousness® I use when I play with the awareness of the future, relates to choice. *If I choose this, what will my life be like in the next five years? 10 years? 50 years? And If I don't choose this, what will my life be like in the next five years? 10 years? 50 years?* You don't look for an answer when you ask these questions. Just notice the energy when you ask both the questions. Which one makes you feel light and expansive and which one makes you feel contracted? Choose based on that. It takes logic out of the equation so you can make choices based on energy and awareness of the future.

"What wisps of awareness do you have right now that you are not listening to, that if you did listen to, would change your entire life and give you what you are asking for?"

Trusting YOU brings more ease and joy into your life and changes your world and everyone else's world around you as well. It allows your brilliance to flow easily and effortlessly. The more vulnerable you are and less barriers you have to receiving information from the future, the closer you get to creating a life that you desire. A life that is fun for you.

Trusting you is one of the greatest gifts you can give to yourself. Trusting you ALWAYS creates more possibilities, never less.

Chapter 6

Being Authentic

One thing I wish I had discovered earlier in life is that fullness of life and an easy, joyful and hedonistic living requires greater and greater amount of vulnerability. In my journey of discovering and exploring this, the key thing I have learned is that vulnerability has a lot to do with receiving myself first, and then from others.

Do I know what it means to be authentic, to be the real you? Yes. Can I define it? No. I wonder if anyone really can define it. To me, it seems more like a state of being, an energy, rather than a definition. It is something that I can perceive and know but cannot describe in words. So how can you know if and when someone is being authentic? Is it because of who or what they are being or because of what they are NOT being?

I started looking at this for the first time when I read Dain Heer's book *"Being You, Changing the World"*, the very first book that introduced me to the tools of Access Consciousness®. Until then I had never heard the term 'Being YOU' and never once in my life had asked the question of myself if I was being me, being authentic. This level of unawareness of me and living in oblivion was the biggest barrier I had created, unconsciously, so that I could remain hidden.

I thought that who I was being was "me", until I got to Dain Heer's book four years ago and realized that in most situations I was either being someone else – like my mother, father, husband, friend or something else – like a victim, control freak, a rebel and so on. Have you noticed that most of us live our lives not for us but for somebody else, based on what people around us want us to be like? My life and reality was determined mostly by other people's judgments than what "I" really wanted. So this awareness of where I was being someone else was the catalyst to my journey of discovering myself.

As I played more with vulnerability and lowered all the barriers I had created to myself, I began to see glimpses of the real me. I am now more willing to show up without filters and that's what authenticity means to me. There are no defense mechanisms and I no longer function from a lie that I need protection and hence the filters. I don't have the need to prove myself to me or to anyone else. Being authentic is to show up as an 'unprotected presence'. It is a conscious choice I make every moment to not have any defense and choose vulnerability instead, with the willingness to be imperfect, to fail, to make mistakes, to mess up, to own up everything I have created – good or bad, without any judgments of it and then choose something different to change it all. There is a huge sense of space, ease and joy with this level of vulnerability! The more I choose it and get freedom, the less I want to go back to my old way of being, with filters.

The experience of exploring vulnerability for me

personally has been very expansive. It has opened me up to all aspects of myself. Being willing to see and share all aspects of myself. Not just the parts of me that I had labelled as nice, beautiful, perfect and lovable. Or the parts of me that I thought other people wanted to see, that if I came across a certain way and people saw me like that then they would like me. More so it was allowing people to see everything about me, even if that meant they disliked me, didn't want to be friends with me or hang out with me anymore, even if they wanted to walk away from my life. When I made this choice and began this journey of choosing for me, many friends and relatives did walk out my life as expected, but I am in total allowance of it and in a place where I don't have the "need" to have anybody in my life.

I made a demand that no matter what, I am choosing "me", every moment. I am fine to let people go but I am not going to give up ME for anyone or anything. Been there, done that all my life. Not doing that anymore. And the result? I am a much happier person today. I am alone but not lonely. Most of us have this belief that being alone is not OK or it is wrong. We are told we always "need" people in our lives. But as infinite beings, the truth is we are all alone, aren't we? But we somehow associate being alone with feeling lonely.

Aloneness is different from loneliness. You can be with a group of people or in a relationship or with your family and yet feel lonely. Loneliness is a state of mind, whereas aloneness is a state of being. With loneliness there is a sense of lack and the "need or necessity" to have someone. If that need is not satisfied then there is a feeling of emptiness within. For instance, I would feel lonely even if I were to be with a group of friends, when I did not get approval or validation from them, because for me, my sense of self-worth came from how much other people liked me and validated me. Now, I am not saying that if you choose vulnerability you will be alone. It's only recently that I realized that most of the people who walked away from my life are those who didn't have my back. They were there until they got something out of me and left when I chose something different and I didn't fit into their expectations. The best part is, now I am surrounded by people who truly have my back and they are a huge contribution to me and towards expanding and growing my life. That's the gift and I am extremely grateful for them! What would your life be like if you had more of this nurturing, caring and kind energy with you? More often than not, it shows up when you choose to be vulnerable.

One of the key aspects of vulnerability for me is the strength and ability to stand up for myself and speak up. To say what is true for me without being apologetic or judgmental. Yes, speaking my truth with others was a part of it, but a greater part was to allow me to see what is true for me. When I say speak, I don't mean it literally always. It is about knowing what works for me and what doesn't and being aware of what "is", not how I expect things to be.

As I have mentioned earlier, I grew up with this crazy need to please others. Saying no to people was the toughest thing for me to do. I felt like people would dislike me if I said no when they asked me for something. I couldn't handle rejection. My point of view was, I would rather do things I dislike and be frustrated than say no and handle being rejected. I've done this insanity in relationships, at workplace, with bosses, clients, colleagues, friends, family, in short, with everyone!

When I lowered these huge concrete walls which were blocking me from seeing all of me, I noticed that I do this insanity. This was only an observation without judging myself as wrong for doing it but simply accept it. Secondly, I asked the question "What would it take for me to change this?" I made a demand of myself that this has to change, as it clearly doesn't work for me. This question and demand changed the heavy energy around it almost instantly. Then I went out in the world and started practicing saying NO to people every time they asked me something and I didn't want to do it. Whatever stuff came up for me after saying no, I simply observed it, let it go, changed it or chose something different. It got easier with practice. There is much more space and joy in my life now to create things that I truly desire to create and it is fun for me and not because I ended up committing to someone due to my stupidity!

I also noticed that when I am willing to be vulnerable as I am saying NO to people, I don't do it from a place of superiority, judgment or to turn them down. It is only about letting them know it doesn't work for me and I am willing to re-look at it if things change in the future. I am not closing the doors. It is not being chosen in that moment, that's it. It creates more space and possibilities for the future. In fact by choosing this level of vulnerability, I have continued to create joyful relationships, personally and professionally. However, there have been a few people, friends and colleagues both, who have been offended by my honesty and they have chosen to walk away from my life. I now know it is about them, not about me. It is a choice they made, not something I judge myself for, like I did in the past. Wow, just writing this gives me a sense of freedom and joy. The true gift of vulnerability!

Being YOU, being authentic, is not defined. It's not even cognitive (which is why you can't define it!). It is something that keeps evolving and changing every moment. It is in fact a choice that you make every moment to be whatever energy you wish to be in that moment. You may show up in different ways but the unique essence of you (like an energetic signature) stays with you. So what you should get is the energy of what it is to be you, a sense of what it feels like and just be aware that you are not living somebody else's life but yours, and only yours.

"What if you could discover YOU and be something different every single day?"

Chapter 7

Unleashing Creation and Creativity

Create or Die seems to be an eternal mandate of nature. If you are not creating, you perish. It is a choice if you want to create something constructive and greater or live life as if you don't exist. I knew I was a great creator because of all the crap and judgments I had created in my life! When I found Access Consciousness® I received the tools to channel my creative capacity in a generative way rather than to create based on judgments and destroy my life. I now see creativity and vulnerability as my superpowers, which I had buried as deep as I could, but they are now the source of all my creations.

"If you are not doing create, which is about stepping into the energy of what is going to generate a possibility in life, what you are doing is trying to maintain what was."
~Gary Douglas

As the author and scientist Brene Brown says – *"Vulnerability is the birthplace of innovation and creativity"*. Without vulnerability you cannot innovate. There is something vulnerable about trying something new. If you are going to try something new that no one else is doing, then the willingness to take risk, to fail, to be uncomfortable and be courageous is very essential. You have to come out of your skin and your objective is not comfort.

Fear and doubt seem to be the key impediments to creation and creativity. The only purpose of these two emotions are to distract you from being who you are! As long as you keep buying into fear and doubt as real and true, you are stuck in a never ending loop of distraction and you never get to see the truth that is underneath it – which is to be vulnerable and embrace courage to be your true self. I lived in this endless loop for 30 years of my life. I had assumed I am not creative because I am not born with that gift. I thought creativity is for the artistic only. A couple of years ago, I would have not even thought of writing a book. Now I know each one of us have that capacity and it is just our choice and willingness to nurture it, unleash, unlock and embody it.

I had no idea that creativity and being vulnerable were connected until I saw my creative abilities explode as I chose to be more of "me" and pushed my barriers down. I realized that the barriers of protection I had around me were preventing me from receiving my own talents, abilities and creative energies. When I dissolved those walls, it felt like flood gates opened and gave me access to an ocean of unlimited possibilities. It is true that creativity demands vulnerability because it's the fuel that feeds creativity.

Creating from a place of vulnerability allows you to reach out to the depths of your being and brings out your inner essence and raw emotions into your book/poem/song/ dance/video or any product you are creating, so that your audience can relate to your experience and get inspired to choose change for themselves.

> *"The power of vulnerability is that it allows us to be authentic. This is a key component of real connection, whether it's through creativity or anything else."*

When you are living in a box with walls all around you, it is obvious that you are blocking all the creative ventures from talking to you. I love what author Elizabeth Gilbert says about the creative genius, that it is something external to you, which has a life of its own and you can talk to it as if you would talk to a person. Creation is not something you do on your own. You collaborate and work with these life forms together to create. For it to occur with ease, you have to be present without barriers to receive the awareness. When I let my guard down and allow my creativity to unleash, there are days when I perceive several tiny sparks of creations trying to communicate with me at the same time, wanting to be manifested in this world. They still do, even today. Some are for now, some for the future. They are very subtle and for me, it requires a lot of vulnerability to receive them. It is mind-blowing to see how things work out with ease when you are vulnerable with your creations.

A great example is this book you are reading. It had been talking to me since December 2014. Initially I ignored it, then the spark got brighter, so I acknowledged it and said ok I'll write a book but didn't do anything much. Then the voice got louder and louder and it would be present all around me while I was awake and asleep, until the time I was willing to receive it completely with my barriers down and take action.

I had absolutely no idea about what it takes to publish a book. It was all Greek and Latin to me and it would bring up a lot of resistance in my world. It was so huge that I couldn't continue writing until I figured this all out. I knew that was crazy and I was asking for it to change. So I told the book exactly those words and asked it to find a publisher if it wants to be born. I put this question out there and let it be. After a few days, I was browsing through Facebook and came across a book I wanted to purchase but it wasn't available in the kindle format and contacted Erica Glessing, who was the editor of it. While we were chatting, I randomly had an awareness to ask her if she does publishing and works with first-time authors and she said yes, let's talk! I had spoken about this book with a couple of people before but when I told Erica about this book she received it very differently than the others, she tapped into the energy of the book instantly. I perceived that is because she herself embodies vulnerability and is one of the sweetest people I know. It felt light and expansive for both of us and the deal was done in the next couple of days! The book had found the most awesome person to create with and thanks to Happy Publishing, this book has reached out to all you readers, the way it intended to!

I'd spend days and weeks lowering my barriers to my creative flow, to know what is it that I am good at that I am pretending not to know. I opened myself to receive all those ideas and sparks of creativity that were shining near me, waiting to be created through me, that I was not even seeing! I realized that my point of view of me not being a creative person born with the gifts, was a lie that I was functioning from. I had these huge walls to prevent myself from listening to these ideas that were talking to me all the freaking time! Suppressing this flow actually created a lot of disease, aches and pains in my body. Not a smart choice I made.

I started going on creative dates with myself, in solitude. I allowed creativity to flow through me and let go of any blocks I perceived. I did this more often. When I opened the dam and let my creative energies burst out and I received and embraced them fully, most of the discomfort in my body disappeared. So my body was also giving me an awareness of this creative block that I was choosing. I am glad I listened to it.

Initially it was overwhelming, to say the least, to have these ideas coming in from every direction. I started keeping a journal listing all these ideas and asking each one of it, if it is for now or for the future. I'd take action only if it is for the present. Future ones can wait, but I don't ignore or forget them as the journal would act as a reminder. This process created more ease. The more I listened and received, the more ideas flowed in, waiting to be discovered. I want to point out something important here. Not all these ideas I received were very clear to me to start with. Most of them were foggy, I could just see a glimmer. I had no clue what to do with it. Many of them are like a seed, they are still germinating, not fully formed. Like the idea of this book. I'll let you in on my little secret here. I just knew a book wanted to be written. I made a note in my journal in December 2014 that was simply "write a book". I didn't know the how, what, when, where and why of it.

As weeks passed by and my life was changing dynamically, I was being different, opening up to new spaces that I had never accessed before, ever. That's when I started getting more information on what I can write about. The fog lifted slowly and when the word vulnerability came up, it felt like it fit in perfectly. The energy matched the book. I could see the book now, it came into existence in my awareness, more cognitively. I trusted it completely. So it takes time for the sparks to become ideas, become cognitive and come into this reality. It's a process of nurturing it with love, care, trust, acknowledgement, so that it grows, matures and flourishes into the magnificence and brilliance that it is capable of.

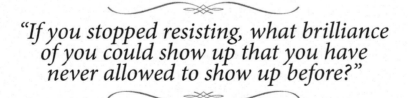

"If you stopped resisting, what brilliance of you could show up that you have never allowed to show up before?"

It is vital to realize that when you are being your true self, that is the magical energy of creation. It creates everything–

money, relationships, business, joy, possibilities etc. in your life. When you are willing to be the magic that you are, without limiting yourself in anyway, creative energy flows through you spontaneously and effortlessly. If you stop stopping yourself and resisting it, you can receive it with ease.

To be vulnerable during the process of creation means you never diminish your ideas or make yourself small in favor of someone else's opinion. There are times when I underestimated my creative capacities because of other people's points of views and judgments of it. What I've found is that I was creating for the future at times and people around me were not ready to receive that yet, they thought I was crazy or invalidated me saying it won't work, it's not true blah and blah and I ended up judging that my ideas were not good.

Let's say you are with a group of people, brainstorming about a venture, it does feel good to flow along with the ideas of the group and build a consensus and align and agree with everyone else so that everyone is happy. But it requires a level of vulnerability and courage to go in a different direction from the group and present an idea that is radically different and innovative. What if you could be that one person who is willing to be aware of the future and show people that a different possibility exists? You can be a leader who is vulnerable enough to be seen as weird and different and leads an entire group towards a wild idea that they didn't know exists.

"What creative capacities and magic do you have that you have not yet acknowledged?"

These sparks come from a space that is beyond our mind. Is it from the future? From a different dimension or another universe? I have no idea and it doesn't matter! When you are vulnerable and willing to let your guard down to access these unknown places and spaces, it is like taking a risk because you have no clue what you will find there. It's not a place you've been before. With that risk and courage to explore the unknown territory comes this joy of creation, creativity, and potent dynamic change that gives you access to unexplored depths of YOU. Isn't it interesting that everything finally comes down to finding more of YOU? It's like all roads lead you there! That's what I am interested in and choosing every single day of my life because it's fun. How about you?

PART
Three

DIVING DEEPER

Chapter 8

Being Vulnerable in Relationships

Everything that I have learnt about vulnerability in relationships is through the process of creating an amazing, kind, caring, nurturing, fun and expansive relationship with my husband and I am extremely grateful for him for stepping up, choosing more of him, playing and creating with me, and for his willingness to explore a possibility of creating a relationship that is beyond the definitions of this reality.

When I met my husband for the first time in the year 2009, at the Dubai airport where he had come to pick me up, one thing that was strikingly obvious and attractive about him was his vulnerability and softness. It showed in his body language, in his smile and his demeanour. Even though that was the first time I was seeing him, I could perceive all of it energetically. Most of us have this capacity to perceive and over years I've come to recognize and acknowledge that I've always had this ability of getting a huge energetic download about people when I first see them. His openness, sweetness and gentleness was remarkable and it still is. Seeing that level of sweetness and caring in a man, especially after having had a couple of terrible and miserable relationships in the past, melted my world. I knew instantly that I wanted to be with him, with that energy. It was also overwhelming as I had always chosen the wrong kind of men in my life and this was first time I was in presence of somebody very different than anyone I had ever met. I let go of my guard and lowered my walls to receive all of that as I spent time with him for the next week.

We were both completely open with each other about our mistakes and insanity from the past, without having any fixed point of view about it. When you don't judge something, it is easy for the other person to drop judgments of it too. Most importantly, we had no judgments of each other and that's what created a beautiful connection between us and we went on to get married after six months.

Everything was not perfect and hunky dory when we got married. There were highs and lows and rough patches to begin with, like in most relationships. What changed it was our willingness to create something greater and different that worked for both of us.

One of the most important aspects of being vulnerable in relationships, in my opinion, is to be your true self, the real YOU where you never give up yourself, your uniqueness, your quirkiness or weirdness for the sake of your partner, no matter what. Gary Douglas calls this a "Divorceless Relationship" which means you never divorce any part of yourself in order to have an intimate relationship with somebody else. You never give up things that are valuable to you, things that make you happy, for the sake of somebody else. Like giving up a favorite hobby of yours because your significant other wants to spend more time with you. You don't tweak, adjust, bend, staple or fold yourself in order to please your partner. This applies for all kinds of relationships, not just a romantic one. Remember that a relationship always begins with YOU.

Imagine, if you are not real and pretending to be someone or something else, then your partner is connecting with someone fake, and not "you". Can the relationship be genuine at all? It's only pretentious. If you lose your originality, your core essence and YOU no longer exist, how can you create a communion with anybody else? Is that even a possibility?

In my opinion, it is equally important for both people in a relationship to express their authenticity. When I started to choose to be more of ME in my marriage, but my husband was still divorcing parts of him, it wasn't fun or easy, for either of us. There were times when I would go into guilt because he wasn't choosing things that would bring him joy. I would feel guilty for putting myself first in every choice I made. None of the guilt was real or true.

I had to stop judging myself and acknowledge that "he" had to choose to be his true self and stop cutting off parts of him. When he made the choice finally, our marriage expanded exponentially and it keeps getting better every day, as we give each other the space and allowance to be ourselves and yet maintain a deep connection and communion between us.

There is no substitute for the real you. So never change your personality to match someone else's expectations. I've been there done that, not just once, but a few times, ready to give myself up at the drop of a hat in order to fit into the other person's needs and I can confidently say it wasn't a smart choice. If you are anything like how I was until five years back, the minute you enter into a relationship with your significant other, your entire life starts to revolve around him/her. You will ensure you meet his/her expectations and needs, and constantly think about ways to make him/her happy. You strive to be the perfect partner they have ever had, and forget "you" in the process.

In all of my previous relationships, I made the other guy's interests my interests because they expected it, or because I wanted to create what a dating magazine calls 'chemistry' between us. I had wrongly assumed the basis of that is to have similar interests. Heck, I even listened to death metal music (that I hated) in my late teens because the guy I was dating loved death metal! It sounds very funny in my head right now but that's how I lived my life back then. I would also jump from one relationship to another very quickly. Having a gap after a breakup meant I got all the time for myself, to take care of my needs, be independent, and I hated that because I loved giving myself away. I was living my life based on other people's projections and expectations of me.

I did not like "me" time because then life would be different. I used relationships as an excuse and distraction to never focus on ME. I was never kind to myself nor did I love myself and I was looking for a partner to give me all of this, as if that would give me respite from the "love yourself" project! Over years of doing it and across several relationships, I finally reached a point where I had absolutely no idea who I really was anymore. It surely didn't create happy or fulfilling relationships and it took me a couple of years to undo the damage and abuse I had perpetrated onto myself!

Honoring your own feelings and desires are part of being vulnerable in a relationship. That means, at some point, say you require your personal space, and don't feel like answering a phone call or email from your significant other, right at that moment, then don't do it. Honor your feelings and desire for space without worrying about how the other person will react. Respond to it when you have the space or be vulnerable and say now is not a good time to talk. It is about speaking your truth, without being apologetic or judgmental about it.

Honoring the other person and being grateful for them is also equally essential. In my opinion, gratitude contributes a lot to vulnerability. When you are grateful to somebody for their contribution and presence, you have no judgments of them. Because gratitude and judgment cannot co-exist. They are mutually exclusive. When you have no judgments, there is less separation and barriers, so you are more open and vulnerable to contributing and receiving from each other. When you honor yourself, you also stop being with people who judge you. You stop being with people who cannot receive you for who you are and those who don't embrace you in all your glory and brilliance.

When you are being with someone who lets you be you and inspires you to keep choosing to be even more of you, your life will grow and expand exponentially, beyond what you can even imagine. I say this from experience and I am beyond grateful that I get to live and create with one such person in my life – my husband.

One thing I always had a huge resistance to, is letting go of things and letting go of people in my life – friends, family and my husband too. Here is what I found. It's what you hold onto and are not willing to let go of a lot of times, or what you are not willing to actually have, that is what controls you and limits the amount of change you can have. It's very vital to me now that I have all of me and my authenticity irrespective of who stays in my life or walks away. I am not giving up "me" for anyone else's sake. Not anymore.

How many of you have somebody in your life you are not willing to let go of? And you know if you change too much you might let go of them or they might not want to be with you anymore. So you won't allow the change to occur because you might lose them. Every time I've been willing to let go of somebody like that from my life, and continue to go in the direction that I was going, what I found is they either come along, step up and become greater or they would simply disappear and vanish out of my life and it never hurt me. How much hurt are you trying to avoid with the people you are trying to stay connected to and the change you are not willing to have? Is it time you give that up now please and let your entire life change?

The truth is, you can never lose the people from your life who truly have your back. They never limit you, pull you down or prevent you from being you or expanding your life. Those who walk away when you choose to be more of YOU, are the ones who probably never had your back anyway but they pretended to as long as they got something from you, when that went away, so did they.

Chapter 9

Being Vulnerable with Your Business

I was always excited about creating a business and being an entrepreneur, which is one of the reasons I got a Masters degree in Business Administration. While in B-school I surely did learn a lot about the way business is done in this reality, the form and structure of it. What I found is missing most of the times is the joy and fun with business. Deep down I knew there is a different way of doing Business but didn't know how, until I took the "Joy of Business" classes with Simone Milasas, the worldwide co-ordinator of Access Consciousness®. I saw how she created her business very differently from the rest of the world and that's what I knew was possible. As I continued using these tools of Access Consciousness®, it expanded my business beyond my imagination. There is more money, more visibility, more clients, and more success, and above all, there is loads of fun and joy. As a business owner, I trust myself completely and don't deny my "knowing" anymore. This level of trust has allowed me to create a lifestyle and business that I've always desired.

*"Your business has
a consciousness of its own.
Are you listening to it
and receiving from it?"*

What I've been exploring over the past five years of creating my business is how to be ME and bring in "my" essence into the creation of my business. I didn't want to give up me or my life in the process of creating a business. As I've chosen to be more vulnerable, it feels as if magically my business has expanded and opportunities have been seeking me rather than me going after them. The energy that I am being seems to be attracting these amazing possibilities into my life and business which I had never expected to come my way.

When it comes to business, we are led to believe that we can't be vulnerable. Most people also believe that if they show their vulnerable side to their clients, employees or partners they will either take advantage of them or not work with them. This is obviously a misconception.

Entrepreneurs benefit a lot from showing vulnerability. When you shut it off, you cannot create deeper connections with people or let them be included in your business. You have to be willing to speak your truth. That doesn't mean you share your deepest, darkest secrets of you or your business. It is about being transparent with your clients and employees and all stakeholders. You don't pretend to be someone or something else in your business or at work. You show up as completely unique as you are. The most interesting thing I noticed is that when I am being me, this allowed my business to change for the greater and it also changed my experience of my business for the greater.

"How many judgments and conclusions do you have about your business that if you let go of them, would expand and grow your business exponentially?"

Are you wondering what being vulnerable with your business looks like? Here is what I have found while I played with my business. It is your willingness to be wrong, to lose everything, to have everything, to change everything, to be judged, to be ridiculed, to have insane amounts of money, to be more successful than anyone you know and to make choices that you know would create something different and greater. It is about choosing what you "know" with business rather than doing things based on other people's point of view about how a business "should" function, just because they have a degree or credibility.

Your awareness is far greater than what anyone else tells you to do. Being vulnerable is your willingness to trust yourself and your business, no matter what. Vulnerability is also about being open to receiving everything. Right now, just take a look at your business for a few seconds. Perceive all the barriers that you have with it. If you had no barriers at all with your business, would you be able to receive more than what you have currently? Receive in a very different way? That would be a yes!

So how do we create barriers to our business? By having fixed points of views, conclusions, expectations and judgments about it. If you didn't have any of that, what would you be able to receive? Just get a sense of that energy. Everything that you have decided your business is, all conclusions you have about your business, lower your barriers and let the conclusions go. Everywhere you have decided what is already right or wrong, when it comes to business, are you ready to give it up? When you are being vulnerable, you don't have to prove anything to anyone, you don't have to get it right or wrong, and there are infinite possibilities available.

Howard Shultz, CEO of Starbucks, once said, "*The hardest thing about being a leader is demonstrating or showing vulnerability. When the leader demonstrates vulnerability and sensibility and brings people together, the team wins.*" Being vulnerable at your workplace doesn't mean you have to share your deepest, darkest secrets with everyone and be in tears. It means you don't have your guard up all the time, you don't pretend to be someone you are not and just be your real self. You as a leader are not looking to create blind followers on your team. You are willing to not have answers all the time, make mistakes, be in allowance of your team members' varied perspectives and opinions and you are willing to inspire people, invite them to a possibility they have never explored before. Your employees, colleagues and your team feel more connected to you and your business/organization and you are also better aware of what is it that they can contribute to and receive from the business. This expands the business/organization as a whole.

So the key elements are:

- Your willingness to trust what YOU know.

- Always be in the question, never go into conclusions. Be open and willing to ask for information and assistance from others if it is required.

- Having a choice every moment. Not making anything a necessity just because you added it in your business plan. Be willing to change it all, even when it will cost you money. Then money can never control you. That will give you the space to never be afraid of having any awareness regarding your business. Especially if you are planning your business way ahead into the future. Nothing is a decision that can't be changed. You don't allow the business plans to limit you. Never! If you are not willing to incur an expense to change your plans and make choices that will create more, you will also not have greater choices showing up in your life. Not every time I make money out of every workshop I facilitate. There are times when I travel to a different country to teach and I don't break even. But I still choose it because there is an energy available there that creates and contributes for the future. At times it has created as far as two years into the future and because

I was willing to trust it and choose it, I've made ten times more money later. Universe always has a way of gifting you, if you are willing to have your own back and trust your awareness. Look at what are you not willing to invest in you and your future because of money? If you limit your choice solely based on money, that will be the most expensive choice you will ever make. Look at the energy of whether the choice will create something more. You will not get a logical proof for it. If you wait for the proof then you have diminished the possibilities and you are not being being vulnerable. You have to be willing to be aware and trust, all the time!

"How different would your business be if you threw your rule book out and followed your awareness?"

Clients and customers are a vital component of your business. People want to get a sense of who you are when they want to work with you, especially in my kind of profession where it is about facilitating people and interacting with them closely. If you are not willing to be vulnerable with them, you cannot create a deeper connection. If you have judgments about them, you cannot contribute anything to or receive anything from them. Judgments create separation. It is a huge barrier. When I started my business, this field of work was very new to me. I used to try my best to create an image with my clients that I am a perfect, good and best therapist. Having this judgment and expectation meant that I didn't have the space to make any kind of mistakes whatsoever. If I did, I had to find ways to cover it up so that I don't come across as incompetent. Being this way drained my energy and I hated it. There was no joy. As I chose to be vulnerable, I was willing to fail and make mistakes without having any judgments of me. There was more freedom in that choice. Interestingly, my clients trusted me more and connected with me better.

This reminds me of an instance a couple of months back. I completely forgot I had given an appointment to someone for an online session. I forgot to put it on my calendar and planned something else in that slot. On that day I realized it only when my client called me at our appointed time. Rather than getting frenzy and judging myself as terrible, I acknowledged I made a mistake and was honest with her that I forgot. It gave her the space to not defend or judge me either. She was very cool about it and we fixed a session another day and I gave her extra time to make up for the damage done. It created so much ease for both of us, didn't spoil our relationship and she loved the fact that I was honest! She also referred a couple of her friends to me. I love what vulnerability can create!

In another instance I had someone call me asking for a Tarot Reading session. Without even a polite hello, he started off with questioning my ability to do these sessions and if I am psychic/clairvoyant to give him the "solutions". He was being very mean and nasty. Previously, I would have my defenses come up instantly, get irritated and I'd get into reaction mode. But I immediately chose to lower my walls and I was completely fine with losing this client (previously, I would have judged myself for saying NO to someone). Very humorously I answered all his questions and at the end told him I am not right person for him. I suggested he find someone else who can give him what he desires because I'd love for him to get the best out of a session. I perceived his barriers melt instantly and his demeanor changed. He became softer and polite and said he still wanted to see me. Even though I didn't give him an appointment he chose to sign up for my workshops. All this happened in a 20-minute conversation with total allowance and vulnerability. Every time I have chosen to be vulnerable with my clients, I have had access to more of me and it has expanded my business beyond my imagination!

Vulnerability with business is to know that your business is a CHOICE. It is not a necessity. You don't "have" to do it or stick to it because you created it in the past. When I wake up every morning and I look at my business I ask, am I doing this out of necessity or is it a choice? If I feel like anything I am doing with my business is coming out of a necessity, for example if I have to see a client just because I have given an appointment but it doesn't feel light or fun for me that day, I ask what can I do differently to make this a choice instead? I might reschedule the session or do something else before the session to nurture myself so I am in a different space or whatever it takes to make it a choice. Also know that there is nothing like a right or wrong choice. That's a judgment we attach. Everything is just a choice and no choice is permanent.

As a lack of vulnerability with business, I noticed a tendency to get into my comfort zone. I wasn't exploring new horizons, taking risks or creating more, thus limiting my potential for growth and success with my business. Being vulnerable brought in the elements of courage, creation and change. Comfort is also largely based on not letting go of control. There is definitely a level of discomfort that comes in when you go out of control. I was not ready for it initially.

Being a huge control freak I wanted to do everything by myself. I wasn't willing to ask for help or hire somebody else to work with me, because I thought no one else could do the job like I do. There were certain parts of the business which, even though I was good at, it wasn't fun for me. The point of view that I had to do it all, created a necessity and frustrated me. When I let go of control, I started asking for somebody to show up, who could do the job way better than I did and who would also be fun to work with. I asked my business to find people who would be a contribution to it. Having these amazing incredible people work with me, expanded my business, created more success and something greater for the future.

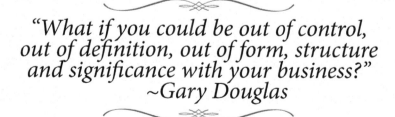

"What if you could be out of control, out of definition, out of form, structure and significance with your business?"
~Gary Douglas

Last but not the least, it's not your degree or credentials

that determines what you can create with your business. It is what you know, how much you trust yourself, how much courage and strength you have to create something that is wild, whacky and different and far beyond your comfort zone and beyond this conventional reality.

Chapter 10

Being Vulnerable with Your Body

Do you know that the thoughts, beliefs, emotions and judgments you hold on to, get locked up in your physical body and determines your body's shape, size and the way it looks and feels? Our point of view about our body creates it exactly like that. Our bodies have consciousness. They are giving us awareness all the time. One of the things that prevents us from receiving this awareness from our body is our own barriers. They are the several judgments that we have about how our body looks, those places where we feel we need to protect or defend ourselves, the invisible walls that we erect between us and others to ensure we don't get hurt and all sorts of things that we have discussed so far.

When we have these barriers in place, we can't receive the information our body is giving us about what, when, where, why and how it requires to eat, drink, sleep, move, exercise, travel etc. We ignore this and override our body's awareness and do things our way based on the fixed points of views and judgments that we have about how we should do things and then when our body doesn't look the way we want it to, we get upset and judge it for not being good! It will look amazing, the way it desires to, only if you are willing to be open and listen to it. When you don't listen to the subtle information that your body is giving you, it tries to turn up its volume in the way of aches, pains or an illness, so that it is heard. That's our body's way of communicating that something needs our attention. Instead of being vulnerable and receiving that information, we continue to judge it for creating pain and illness too. That's the insanity we create.

That being said, communicating with our body and listening to what it has to say may not come overnight. I drove myself crazy initially when I didn't get it. It almost felt like I found another reason to judge my body that it doesn't communicate with me. This is a muscle that you build. It requires practice. You have to treat it like a dear friend and gradually build an intimate relationship based on trust, gratitude and respect. Also, the communication is not cognitive or logical, as you expect. Most of the times it is just an energy, a knowing. Very subtle. Goes beyond words. So it's like learning a new language – the language of energy. It took me several months to get it, as I lived in my head most of the time than my heart. So I had to give up my mind and follow my knowing. That's when I started getting it.

Our bodies are naturally vulnerable when we are born. It is receiving information from everything around, all the time. If someone in your family has a headache, your body might give you a sensation of headache as an information. But we may put up a barrier if we think the information can be uncomfortable. Instead ask questions like: Body, what awareness are you trying to give me? What am I not receiving here? What do we need to do different to change this? As long as you are asking questions of everything showing up in your body, then you are willing to receive the information. That's being vulnerable.

Just like vulnerability is a key element to create an intimate relationship with somebody, it is a key element to create an intimate relationship with your body as well. With vulnerability comes a lot of caring, sweetness, gentleness, trust and kindness to your body. How many people do you know who actually take time out to nurture their body, as often as it requires?

I never did that, all my life. I never recognized how aware my body was and how much healing capacity it had, ever since I was a kid. Because I had learnt to put my guard up to protect myself, I resisted this information all along. Then I would wonder why I fall sick very often and I would judge my body for not being healthy. I'd try to find justifications that it was because of a lack of a proper diet or exercise or my lifestyle. None of that was true. When I let go of my defenses and pushed my barriers down, I was willing to listen to my body for the first time than tell it what to do. The more I allowed myself to receive all the information my body was giving me, rather than resist it or block it, there was more ease and space in my body. I didn't fall sick often anymore.

It's not only resistance to your body, but any barrier you have to all sorts of things, in every area of your life, gets locked up in your body and it contracts. The more you come out of the hiding, give up all stuff that you are holding onto but not working for you anymore, you release it from your body as well and it blossoms out like a beautiful flower.

I used to judge my body a lot about the way it looked, in every aspect. My body is very petite and I disliked it for most part of my life, and I judged it for not being tall. I had decided somewhere that being tall was better. It's only when I brought my barriers down, and opened myself up to my body did I realize how unkind I was being to myself. Even though my body wanted to look different, it couldn't, because of the judgments I was dumping on it every single day. It had no choice but to create itself to match my judgments. When I finally asked my body, "Body, what would you desire to look like?", it got the space it always wanted, to create itself the way it wants. It's like someone finally giving you the freedom and space to be who you are. I let go of all the resistance I had to look beautiful and attract people's attention to my body and to embody my sensualness.

Ever since then, my body has been changing, altering shape, size and looks, dynamically. People say I look very different than what I was even a month ago. And that I even look taller with my presence, than what I am. My dressing style has changed drastically as I now allow my body to take me shopping and pick the clothes and accessories that it desires to wear. It surprises me by picking up stuff that I would have never worn before. Because of the beautiful intimate relationship that I've been able to create with my body, I am willing to trust every awareness it gives me. More and more people have acknowledged in the past six months as to how beautiful and gorgeous my body looks. I felt good, different and more at ease but I didn't recognize the changes cognitively until I received these comments from others. I am so grateful for these people who acknowledge the changes because they have been a huge gift in bringing these changes to my awareness so that I can choose more of it and even describe it here to you!

I mentioned about receiving in the beginning of this chapter, that our body receives information all the time. As I explored receiving further, I've been amazed and mind blown to discover the level of receiving that our bodies are capable of, when we open ourselves to it. This has been true for me especially with receiving from this planet and nature. That's something I had never even thought of as possible, few years back. Receiving from the earth, plants, trees, oceans, land, buildings etc.? What's that? I wondered until I experienced it.

Have you ever walked into a forest or any place in nature and felt an instant sense of peace and calmness flow all over you, felt your body at ease and full of space, molecules within you tingle and dance and a sense of joy engulf you and this planet? That's receiving the nurturing energy from nature, from this beautiful planet. As I've travelled all over the world, I've seen how much every piece of land across different countries has contributed to my body and towards expanding my life. My body always gives me awareness on which place to travel to on a vacation or for business. I've always trusted that. There are certain places I visited like Machu Pichu in Peru and Kamakura in Japan where my body felt so different and the energy of the land very unique, unlike any other places I've visited in the past. I opened myself to receiving the space, joy and the gifts that the earth there had to offer and I've come home and seen my entire life transform and my body look very different. There are several other places all over the world that have contributed to my body and my life this way and still continues to even today. I am immensely grateful for this beautiful planet for showing me and my body what receiving truly means.

Another vital thing for me in creating an intimate relationship with my body has been the element of gratitude. As I had always judged my body, obviously I was being very ungrateful and had taken it for granted. When I recognized this, I practised being grateful for it more often, like saying a simple 'Thank you' every morning I wake up. Acknowledging the amazing gift my body has been to me all my life and being grateful for it. Every time a judgment came up, I'd replace it with gratitude instead. The more I chose to be grateful, my barriers dissolved even more. There was more space for vulnerability.

It is very interesting that when I chose to be more authentic and show up as my real self and be vulnerable in every area of my life, my body has shifted and altered the most, reflecting those changes at a physical level. I look at my body differently today. I interact with it very differently. I receive from it differently. I communicate with it, I trust it and I am extremely grateful for it. I let my body run the show, almost all the time. There are still times when I do the insanity of judgments but it doesn't stay for longer than few minutes. There is more ease, happiness, space and lots of change! I know this is only the tip of the iceberg and just the beginning of the change that is available and I am still exploring, how much more can I turn it up and what other magic is possible with my body, my life and more!

Chapter 11

Being Vulnerable with Money

Money is always an interesting subject to talk about. I've never had shortage of money in my life, but I always felt like I could have a lot more of it and also more ease, joy and possibilities around it. It's only when I quit my well paying full-time job five years ago and started my own business, I started to look at what my financial reality is. Even though my husband supported me with the initial investment for the business, I wanted my business to create more money and be self-sustained. This was not easy at the beginning, having a new business in a new country where I knew absolutely no one. I was used to having a regular monthly income, being independent and having financial security. Here I was, living in uncertainty and not being able to generate money on a regular basis. I loved my work and my business, but the money aspect did drive me crazy and I was starting to go down the rabbit hole. I was very sure of my decision to quit my job and do what I love doing, but I

119

also wanted to create a different financial reality for myself. What I had, was clearly not working for me anymore. That's when I came across the tools of Access Consciousness® and I am extremely grateful for this as it revolutionized my financial reality.

It's only when I started asking questions around money that I recognized I was functioning from a 'lack' mindset even though I didn't really have lack of money in my life. I also believed I had to work hard to earn money and save most of it for the future. Both these points of views came from my parents and extended family, something I had bought into at a very young age, not cognitively. Letting go of these beliefs changed the foundation of my financial reality.

As I played with being vulnerable in different areas of my life, I explored it with respect to money as well. It's very interesting to see that the more courage and strength I've chosen, the more I've stepped into being my true self, the more it has changed my money situation!

"What if you being your real authentic self could make you more money? What if you could get paid for just being you?"

What does being vulnerable with money look like? Here is what I've found.

HAVING CHOICE WITH MONEY

When you don't have walls or barriers around you regarding money, you always have choice with money – the way you spend it, on what you spend, how much you spend, how much you wish to invest, whether you want to have lots of money or not! It is just a choice. What do I mean by barriers with money? Any fixed points of views, judgments, expectations, conclusions, resistance or beliefs you have about money becomes a barrier. The point of view I had about working hard to earn money was a huge barrier. It meant I couldn't receive money in any other way easily in my life other than working hard. That's how it becomes a barrier to receiving more. That point of view was not even mine to begin with! It was something I had bought from others.

As Gary Douglas, the founder of Access Consciousness® says, 99 percent of our thoughts, feelings and emotions don't belong to us. We buy into it from other people and make it as ours and create our life based on that. That one tool made me realize that almost all points of views I had around money were not mine. I was actually living somebody else's financial reality, not mine! I wonder what would change if you asked yourself "Whose financial reality am I creating? Mine or someone else's?" And if you were to create your financial reality, what would it be like? What would be different? Try it out!

For me, as I long as I have joy, ease and choice with money and I am not making money a "necessity" or a "need" I know I am having my financial reality. When you function from "need" for money, firstly it takes choice out of it. Then money becomes the controlling factor. Secondly, if you make anything a "need" in your life, you go into judgment of it and you if the money doesn't show up the way you expect and within a specific timeline that you want. So you can't create based on your awareness anymore.

Here is my favorite excerpt from *How to Get out of Debt, Stay out of Debt and Live Prosperously*, one of the best books I've read on money.

> *"Once you recognize that you always have choices in the way you spend your money, that you are constantly choosing, you'll begin to make more pleasing and satisfying choices. And the feeling that you can't afford to do or have the things that you want will begin to fall away. If you truly desire something, then eventually you'll find ways to shift your money around and to bring more in, to the point where you can make the choice to have it. There is very little that you HAVE to do with your money. It's mostly a matter of what you CHOOSE to do with it."*

BRUTAL HONESTY WITH MONEY

This was a key element for me as I had assumed that I am willing to have lots of money. I wasn't. Not all the time at least. If I was willing, I would have loads and loads of money right? So I was clearly lying to myself. It took me a lot of vulnerability with myself to be open and brutally honest to see this aspect about me. When it came to charging my clients for sessions or workshops, I was not willing to increase my rates. I thought if I did, no one would pay, but the truth is I wasn't willing to have lots of money in my life. This was one of the ways I ensured I didn't earn more.

There are many who think money is evil, they hate money and then they wonder why they are not having more of it in their life. Well, if you hate something, would you let more of it come into your life? It's only when you are honest with yourself and see that you have these insane points of view that you can begin to change them. I believed having more money came with a lot of problems and also that I didn't deserve it if I didn't earn it myself, through hard work. If someone gifted it to me, it came through inheritance or any other means, I wasn't willing to receive it completely. I had hidden all these points of views from myself for as long as I know, which is why I couldn't change my financial situation much. When I allowed myself to see every single solitary point of view I have about money, no matter how crazy, weird and insane it is, without having to judge me for it, I was able to let it go, choose something different and invite loads of money into my life.

RECEIVING MONEY WITH EASE

Being vulnerable increases your capacity to receive because you are not having armors or walls around you that block things from coming in to your life. The more vulnerable you are, the more money you receive. What if receiving money is as easy as breathing air? Have you ever considered that as a possibility? As Gary Douglas says, it's never about the money. It is always about our willingness to receive that determines how much money we have. The more I've let go of my barriers, more I've chosen to be authentic and received the greatness that I am, more money has been flowing effortlessly into my life. When you choose to receive your greatness, it means you have no issues with being seen as who you really are. When you are being unkind to you by not acknowledging your greatness, receiving your gifts and all other aspects of you, you are creating blocks to not just money but everything else in your life and work. So it is not surprising at all that when I was rejecting myself, pretended I am weak, believed the lie that I had no gifts or potency, I had less money and when I have embraced all of me, I am more than willing to be seen as weird, different and unconventional, I am receiving loads of money!

WILLINGNESS TO ASK FOR MONEY

I know many people who have issues with asking for money from others. I used to be that way too. Even if it was the money I had lent to somebody, and I had to ask for it, my barriers would go up instantaneously. I'd rather not have my money back than go through the discomfort of asking for it. There were also times when friends would want to book a session with me and they would not talk about paying me for it and I'd be extremely uncomfortable asking them to pay. Can you imagine how much receiving I was cutting off by being this way? Once I recognized it, I practiced asking for money in every situation. Every time a barrier of discomfort came up, I simply observed it and pushed it down. I let go of the points of view of what the other person will think about me if I asked for money and I was willing to receive their judgments about me. I also recognized the contribution that "me" and my sessions are to people and I stopped discounting myself. It was the beginning of stepping up, honoring me and acknowledging my abilities. Gradually it became easier to ask for it and my financial situation transformed.

HAVING TOTAL AWARENESS ABOUT MONEY

If you wish to create loads of money, you've got to educate yourself about money and everything that's got to do with it. If you have barriers or resistance to any of it, then you are limiting your financial reality. When I started my business in Singapore I didn't have any idea about filing taxes, various tax laws, accounting, investments, etc. You get the point! What was fun for me was to facilitate workshops and sessions for clients, but all these other aspects of my business would overwhelm me. I had a huge resistance to handling it all by myself as I own a sole-proprietorship. It was just me, with no help. I know that resistance was stopping me from expanding and being successful and it was limiting the money I could have. I chose to break out of these barriers, rather than let them stop me, I educated myself with every aspect around money and finances for my personal life as well as my business. There is a lot more ease with it and it opened up my money flows. Now nothing overwhelms me. I know that if I have a huge resistance, I am not willing to receive something. So all I do is bring down the walls and look at what is required to change it.

Last but not least, what if all the barriers you have that are preventing you from being open and vulnerable with money are not even yours? What if you are buying other people's barriers about money as yours and imitating them to create your financial situation as it is currently? You giving up your barriers about money and choosing to be the real you, opens up the doorways to creating a different financial reality beyond your imagination.

Chapter 12

Vulnerability and Receiving

Before I start talking about vulnerability and receiving, you might be wondering what is receiving? In simple words, for me receiving is all about allowing everything to flow into my life easily without having to resist it, judge it, analyze it or reject it. In total acceptance and allowance of everything. Just like a rock in a stream. As the water flows, the rock is undeterred. It does not resist the stream or get washed away but in complete allowance of the flow of water.

If you notice carefully, the easy flow in receiving is possible only if there are no blocks. If there is any barrier in the stream, the flow is cut off. That is exactly how and why vulnerability and receiving are tied together. If you have barriers around you, for whatever reason, you are cutting off your overall receiving in life. The point is, to receive, you have to be vulnerable. You must open yourself up to the universe and people around you. Trust that the universe will provide everything when you ask and you have to be open to receiving it.

GIFTING AND RECEIVING

Interestingly for me, giving came more easily than receiving. I grew up learning that "it is better to give than to receive". It is also something that I learned from spirituality and metaphysical modalities, that giving is superior to receiving. Most of my life has been spent with barriers to receiving. How many of us already have a lot in our life and we are not yet willing to receive it and we keep asking for more to show up as if we lack something? Being grateful and acknowledging what you already have is the first step to opening up to receive more. When you are truly happy with what you have, and ask the universe for more of it to show up, the universe is happy to gift to you. Giving and receiving are two sides of the same coin. In any interaction, there is a gifting and a receiving – it is a two-way street. Also this interaction cannot occur between two people if either one of them has a barrier. Have you ever been in a relationship where one person is giving all the time and the other person is receiving all the time? How did that make you feel? Were you happy? Was that contributing to you and expanding your life? That would be a NO!

Let's look at another aspect of this. Have you ever gifted something to someone who was not open to receiving your gift or had a barrier to receiving it and it made you feel heavy and uncomfortable? It reminds me of all those times when I was given a gift and I felt like I was obligated to give a gift in return. If someone gave me a compliment or appreciated me, I used to feel like I was obligated to compliment them in return or wonder if they were doing this with an agenda, or if they wanted something from me. Truly I was not being grateful for everything I was being gifted.

One of the reasons why we would do this is because of the stupid expectations we build. We expect things to come to us in a certain way and if it shows up in a completely different way, we don't receive it or at times don't even notice it! What if whenever you are gifted with something, you lower your barriers, be totally vulnerable and wholeheartedly accept it and receive it with gratitude, with no obligation or agenda whatsoever? That would truly expand your life and that of the person who is gifting you. I now choose to say YES! And THANK YOU! for everything that I receive no matter how bizarre it sounds in my head. How much more could you receive from the Universe if you functioned from this space of vulnerability? Can you tap into that energy and get a sense of it? What if you can choose it NOW?

Somehow, somewhere I had decided that 'giving' is an easy thing to do; it is safe and it does not expose me. Receiving on the other hand makes me feel vulnerable and it is true. Because when you are receiving everything 100 percent, you cannot do it behind a barrier. You are exposing yourself to the world around you. People can see who you truly are – the good, bad and ugly of you. It's not easy, I agree but hey, that's what creates possibilities! The more I open myself up to receiving these days, the more I feel satiated, grateful and blessed.

RECEIVING OTHERS

As I explored this more I realized that I functioned from a belief (that's a barrier by the way) that in order to

129

get something done properly, I had to do it all by myself. I was a control freak of magnitude. So I used to be a one-stop shop and ended up doing 'everything' myself and never felt comfortable asking for help or receiving from others. I have tapped into various aspects of this over the past few months and consciously lowered my barriers to receiving from others and chose to be more out of control. I now understand that just because I am vulnerable and ask others for assistance it doesn't mean that I can't do that job. It is just that there are people who can do it better than me and it is more fun for them to do it, so why not allow people to contribute and add to my life if that is going to expand my life and make it way better than I can ever imagine? This feels much lighter than being closed and in control!

RECEIVING AWARENESS

One of the greatest gifts of vulnerability for me is that I started receiving more awareness about everything. I am now able to notice and see things more clearly around me and access more of my intuition or a sense of 'knowing'. Most of the times these things are not cognitive, solid or substantial and they do not make logical sense. But when you are truly vulnerable without any confines or barriers around you, you have access to every kind of information in this universe. You have an all-round or 360 degree awareness of everyone and everything in this world and beyond. What you do with this awareness and how you use it is completely up to you. It can be overwhelming at times, at least initially which why most people feel vulnerability is scary or uncomfortable. It can be uncomfortable because you are now aware of every piece of information that exists around you as you are no longer shutting off your full spectrum awareness with a filter or a barrier. But one key thing to note here is that not all awareness you have is about you. Not all of it belongs to you. It could be of someone else or something else on this planet because each one of us is extremely psychic and just because you have awareness it doesn't mean you have to do something about it. You can simply receive that information, notice it, acknowledge what it is and let it flow and drift through you without having to lock it up in your space. Like the wind blowing.

Being vulnerable and opening up to receiving has allowed me to get out of my comfort zone and step into the magic and the bounty of love and possibilities the Universe is offering.

Questions you can ask:

- **Who can I ask for assistance today that would make this task easy?**
- **Who or what can I add to my life today that would expand my life exponentially?**
- **What am I avoiding by not choosing to receive?**

PART
Four

THE 30-DAY
VULNERABILITY CHALLENGE

About the Challenge

In February 2015, I created a 30-day vulnerability challenge, an online class, and there were 35+ people playing with it. The purpose of creating the challenge was for me to personally explore what it would be like if I chose vulnerability consciously, every single day for 30 continuous days. I wanted to see how that can change my life. Also when you do something daily for 30 days it becomes a habit and part of you. So it gets easier for you to be it even after that.

This section has the daily exercises which I had created for myself to play with for 30 days. I shared these with participants on the vulnerability challenge group and they served as a prompt for people to play with every day and open up the space to be more vulnerable.

This is not work and it is not a necessity that you have to do and keep up with it. It's included here for you to play with, if it is fun for you and if you think you need a reminder every day and you don't know which direction to head or where to begin.

Even though it is a 30-day challenge, it is completely fine if you lag behind and miss a few days. That's part of being vulnerable. What if it is completely fine to slack? Just because it is a challenge you have taken up, doesn't mean you have to force yourself to stick to it. So what if you could give yourself the liberty to lag behind and have the choice to not be vulnerable few days? Do you notice just saying this brings in a sense of lightness and joy?

Please know, the purpose of this is to have fun. The change and everything else comes as a by-product!

Day 1

What would it take to increase your awareness of your barriers? Vulnerability is living without barriers or walls. It is about being comfortable in your own skin, being completely fine with who you are without having the need to change yourself to fit into someone else's expectations of you. It is like walking out totally naked in front of the world without having to hide anything or any part of you. But the purpose of the barriers that we create is to "hide" us.

When you are exploring this, it helps if you know when your barriers come up. These occur so quickly and almost unknowingly (most of the times not cognitive) that it requires you to be mindful to know when you pull up these walls. Resistance is also a form of barrier. Anywhere you are resisting something you have a huge barrier around you. Spend all of today simply noticing when you put up your guard up. What makes you bring up your defenses and armor? Become aware of the 'trigger points' that make you want to reach out and create a fence so that no one has access to you. It may happen when you talk to a particular friend

136

or a family member or your spouse or kids, when you are at work, when you are dealing with money, with your body, with your creativity or when you have to show up in front of an audience. You get the point? Make a note of these trigger points and just ask what would it take to change this? What can I do different here?

Day 2

BARRIERS FREE DAY

Continuing from yesterday, now that you are aware of when you put up your barriers, spend today practicing to lower the walls every time they come up. I don't personally use the words pushing the barriers down, because for me pushing requires effort. But use whatever works for you. What if you can choose to gently let those walls down, allow them to melt dissipate or dissolve? What works for you better?

Are you willing to have the next 24 hours completely barriers free? I wonder what would that create for you?

What incredible things will you begin to receive then? What magic can show up in your life? For a few days, just because it was fun for me, I used a "Mindfulness Bell" app on my phone that rings a bell every one hour and I would go "Do I have any barriers up?" Do what is fun for you!

What if letting down barriers can be FUN?!

Day 3

Watch this Ted Talk by Brene Brown on "The Power of Vulnerability": http://bit.ly/BreneOnVulnerability

If you have watched this already, I highly recommend seeing it again. There are very few people who have talked about vulnerability as a strength, and Brene Brown is one of my favorites. I love her research and her work. I find her absolutely brilliant! I wonder what awareness this video can give you. What other doorways to vulnerability does this open up for you?

Day 4

Vulnerability is about being YOU and it means when you are being you, you are very aware of what you truly desire and what is true for you. So today, what would it take for you to honestly acknowledge what is true for you? What works for you and what doesn't? Whether it is in relationships, with family, friends, in your business, with your finances or with your body.

Are you willing to SPEAK UP TODAY AND ACKNOWLEDGE WHAT IS TRUE FOR YOU?

I was in my hometown visiting my family, and my in-laws stay in a different city, a seven-hour drive away. I had just come home from a long travel and an intense class and I had to acknowledge that it doesn't work for my body to travel again. So as a kindness to me, I chose not to visit them, even if it means they are upset with me for not going. But there was so much ease in my body after choosing to be honest with me and them! This is courage to acknowledge what works for you and what doesn't and not give up YOU for anyone else.

Watch this amazing video, an interview of a Bollywood celebrity/actor. It is vulnerability in action! I love the way this lady has spoken her truth, with honesty, courage and vulnerability on National Television, being a very famous celebrity without bothering about how people or media will judge her for what she says! She is SPEAKING HER TRUTH! And just this vulnerability makes her very attractive!

http://bit.ly/VulnerabilityInAction

Day 5

Do you dare to go naked today?!

Well, I didn't mean it literally (but you can, if that's fun for you!).

Vulnerability is being like an open wound, with no scab, no covering, nothing to hide. Are you willing to be totally naked today? It means, be without any masks or a facade, not creating a pretentious image or hiding any part of you, nothing about you is made a secret. You show up the way you are.

How naked are you willing to be today in front of the world? Every time you speak to someone today, strip yourself off your barriers, pretenses, judgments, conclusions, expectations, and the need for approval from them. JUST

SHOW UP! BE YOU!

The thing that stops us from being totally naked is the lie of rejection that we buy into. No one can reject you, except you. So today when you show up and someone doesn't like you the way you are, don't diminish yourself or make yourself smaller to fit into their box of expectations.

The more raw and naked you be the more you can harness your strengths! Everywhere you have concluded that when you go naked in front of the world you only have to show the bad and ugly parts of you, can you destroy and uncreate that?

I wonder how much of you will come out of the closet today? What aspects of you have you hidden that you are not even aware of? What magic can you unhide today?

Day 6

Did you know that vulnerability makes you attractive and irresistible to others? I have been lucky to come across a few people (men and women) who embody vulnerability to the core of their being, so much so that every molecule in their body vibrates with vulnerability! And I have noticed how irresistible they are because of that and how easy it is for them to get anything they desire. Just by being around them, your life can change.

After I started playing with this, I have noticed how much my body has shifted. I have been hearing from people how beautiful, how sexy and irresistible my body looks (I had to really lower my barriers to fully receive these comments and acknowledge it myself!). Life has become easy with people willing to gift and contribute to me, my business is expanding, more money flowing in, and so forth.

So what if you played with embodying vulnerability today to be an irresistible invitation for people, your business, money, body, and more? You can add in some sensualness too and see what you can create today. I wonder what new doorways can open up for you?

Day 7

UNLOCK, UNWIND, UNLEASH

Vulnerability means being AUTHENTIC, being YOU. When you bring those barriers down, you start showing up as YOU. But how well do you know yourself, I mean really know YOU? The first essential aspect of having a more authentic life is to know what it means to be YOU.

It took me a couple of years to actually get to know what being ME feels like. It is more of an energy and not something that one can define cognitively. Here is a fun exercise. Imagine tomorrow morning you wake up and there is no one else on this planet, except you. Everything else is present, like nature, animals, infrastructure and so forth, but no people, except you. You are all alone on this planet. What would you choose then? Who would you be? What would you do?

The exercise above helps in finding out what it means to be YOU because most of what we think we are is a definition of us projected by others or expectations from our parents, family, friends, culture, religion, society etc. We don't even realize that we are living for others and not for us. What if you could be without any definitions?

Being YOU is not defined. It's not even cognitive (which is why you can't define it!). It is something that keeps evolving and changing every moment. But what you should get is the energy of it, what it feels like and be aware that you are not living someone else's life.

What if you could discover YOU and be something different every single day?

Day 8

ACKNOWLEDGE, BE GRATEFUL AND CELEBRATE!

One thing I have noticed over years is that the more you acknowledge the change in you, the more you can receive it. It is so very vital to be grateful for what you are already receiving and ask for more of that to show up. That is when the universe goes "Oh, you love that? Here is more of it!" It's not just about being grateful for what is showing up, but being grateful for YOU for having chosen vulnerability, having chosen to not have barriers, to unlock your limitations, to go beyond what you never imagined was possible! The more you are grateful, the more magic you can create.

So today, spend the entire day acknowledging everything that has changed for you in the past 7 days of this challenge. Please don't judge that the change has to be huge or significant. It can be very subtle and subtle ones go unnoticed and unacknowledged by us. So be aware of the tiniest of the changes this past week. Look at

- What has been different in your life?

- How are YOU different?

- What have you received?

- What have you chosen different?

- How was has your life shifted? (Changes need not be manifested yet, acknowledge the energetic shifts, the way you feel different)

EXPLORING VULNERABILITY
WITH YOUR BODY

I travel a lot, sometimes three weekends a month. There are times when I ignore my body during travels and I don't pay attention to how tired and sick I feel. When I dropped my barriers and I was willing to listen to my body I got so much information, one of which is my body was screaming for rest, love, care and rejuvenation. I was refusing to give it that. So my choice now is to have a lot of allowance for my sweet body and honor its request.

I am not going to describe what vulnerability with body looks like. What if you explore and play with it for next 24 hours and see what it looks like for you?! It can be different for each one of you and how much more awareness can we open up with our bodies today?!

HEDONISM WITH YOUR BODY!

Apparently exploring vulnerability with bodies is going beyond just 24 hours!

What if today as you are being vulnerable with your body, you can choose to receive pleasure from *everything*?! While eating, walking, drinking, exercising, being sick, working, doing household chores, cooking, dancing, sitting, standing, breathing air etc?!

- How much pleasure can your body receive today from everything you be and do?

- Discover what brings pleasure to your body today!

- How much FUN can you have today with all of this?

Even when I am unwell, my automatic response would be to fight it, resist it. Instead now I look at being vulnerable with my body and I ask "What would it to take to be in allowance of this illness and have fun with it?"

I immediately sense ease in my body and I recover faster. Lowering barriers can surely create magic! The more vulnerable I be with my body, the more pleasurable it becomes.

 **Day 11**

VULNERABILITY WITH MONEY

Today we are going to explore vulnerability with MONEY. I feel like this will go on for more than a day.

Imagine money to be Mr. or Miss. M. What would it be like if you had no barriers when you interact with M?

- What kind of an intimate relationship could you create with M?

- If there were no judgments in this relationship at all, how different would it be?

- What if you could contribute to and receive from M with ease?

Maybe you can spread all the cash on bed, roll on it naked like a baby and see if that dissolves all the barriers you have with money? Remember to have fun discovering what vulnerability with money looks like.

Day 12

Have you been exploring vulnerability with money? We continue doing that today as well.

What does vulnerability with money look like to you? (Make a note of everything that comes up when you ask this question).

For me some of the key things of being vulnerable with

money is about:

- HAVING CHOICE - you always have choice with money, you never make money a necessity.
- RECEIVING MONEY WITH EASE
- ASKING FOR MONEY FROM PEOPLE - If you are someone who has difficulty doing that, practice saying "Can I have the money now please" until you get comfortable doing it.
- YOU HAVE FULL KNOWLEDGE ABOUT MONEY, FINANCES, INVESTMENTS, TAXES and everything that has got to do with money. If you have barriers or resistance to any of it, you are limiting your financial reality.

Lastly, how many people's beliefs about money are you buying into as yours?

How many people's barriers with money are you imitating to create your current financial situation?

If you could have YOUR own reality with money, what would it be? What would it look like?

Day 13

How about choosing vulnerability with you and others and everything else today to GET OUT OF YOUR COMFORT ZONE?

How many of you create your nice, soft, cushy, comfort zone in different areas of your life and erect barriers around it so that you can continue to live there forever and never choose beyond it? And then you keep wondering why you can't create a phenomenal life? One thing I have learned is to always choose something that makes me uncomfortable. That's where I have seen the maximum change for me and some amazing things getting created in my life. Every time I sense discomfort I know there is a huge resistance to change from me and if I choose to be vulnerable there, the result is always what I desired to create. Are you willing to take up this challenge today for real and do it? It may bring up crap for you – that's the point. This is an opportunity to clear it out.

THE FIRST STEP IS TO NOTICE WHERE YOUR COMFORT ZONE IS. Then lower your barriers and choose to go beyond it.

For today, take at least one or more things that you always avoid and resist because that pushes you out of your comfort zone. Now choose it with total vulnerability and see what gets created. Every time resistance comes up, lower those walls and choose vulnerability instead. It's a muscle that you build, keep at it!

It can be simple things too. For example, I hate calling people to invite them for my classes. I don't enjoy socializing and chatting over phone. But I choose to call at least five people today and invite them for my upcoming classes. I used to hate going for networking events where I didn't know a single solitary person. I have pushed myself beyond my comfort zone and have gone there and spoken to strangers and made contacts which contributed to growing my business.

What are you going to choose differently today?

147

Day 14

I was reading a book related to vulnerability and it said you should "Celebrate your Imperfections". That has never worked for me in my life. When you are already in judgment of something and have a fixed point of view about it, and you are trying to use a positive affirmation or 'celebrate it' you seem to be reinforcing the same point of view as real and true!

So what if, you could lower your barriers today and look at the good, bad and ugly – ALL of you, without any veils or filters?

What have you decided are your imperfections and weaknesses? What is the worst judgment you have of YOU which you feel if you shared with people, they would leave you and never talk to you?

Once you become aware of all of this, next ask these questions:

What if everything you have decided is a weakness is actually a gift?

What if everything you have judged as a wrongness of you is actually your strength?

Day 15

I can understand that it can sometimes be exhausting to play, to do this challenge, and constantly be aware not to have barriers around you because it is not something we are used to. Having barriers, protecting ourselves, not receiving, not being aware, having judgments etc., feel more natural to us. So this may seem like an effort. Phew!

What if today we do a "slack day"?! You can choose to have all your barriers (or not!) You have total choice to not be vulnerable today or indulge in resistance, judgments, pretenses whatever (or not!). Observe what this choice creates for you. Choice always gives you awareness. Once you have the awareness, then you can choose something different tomorrow!

Being vulnerable is not a necessity. It is a choice. What if you could have the freedom today to be vulnerable or not and indulge in every type of experience just because you can?

Day 16

After an easy slack day, let's explore vulnerability through WRITING. For me, writing has been a way of expressing myself and my vulnerability. Today's exercise is to write something and share it with the world. You can write a piece of article, a blog post, a poem, a story or anything that interests you and post it on the Internet or anywhere on social media where people will find it.

How many of you hold back from sharing your creative writings just because you think people will judge it, judge you? When you write, how much do you hold back? How many filters do you use in choosing the words you write and thoughts you express?

Are you being authentic and getting your voice out into

the world when you bother about judgments and do it with barriers around you?

Today, write/share something you would usually never write about because of the fear of judgments. WRITE WITHOUT FILTERS OF WHAT YOU CAN OR CAN'T SAY. Lower your barriers and let go of all the judgments while you write as people will pick that up energetically when they read it.

You can write about ANYTHING you desire! If you don't know what to write, write about your experience doing this challenge and what it has created for you! The point here is to STEP OUT AND SHOW UP in the world, in front of people. What if you could inspire others to choose something greater today?

What if you can bring out your VOICE, your ESSENCE, your vulnerability into the world today through writing?

Day 17

If you did yesterday's challenge then great job! If you couldn't then I am continuing it for today and adding something more to it! You have 24 more hours to play with it.

If you don't have anything to write about, Share a painting, sketch, photos you have clicked or create a video.

Is NOW the time to dissolve the blocks you have to your creative self? Is it time to come out of the hiding? What if you could share your creativity, your voice, your essence with the world without having to seek approvals & validation from people? And judgments don't matter to you anymore?

What if you could include YOUR BODY in your creative work today?! (When you are writing an article, poem, painting, creating videos or photographs, ask your body to contribute to it.) How would your body be nurtured as you let go of those barriers you have to creativity?

Day 18

Receiving is one of the key elements of vulnerability. If you are not willing to receive something it means you have a barrier to it and you are not being vulnerable. So how many of you are asking for more vulnerability and truly open to receiving that when it shows up no matter how it looks like?! When you have an expectation of how something should show up, you create a resistance to receiving it as well.

Today let's play with receiving. Let's deepen our receiving by choosing more vulnerability and see what shows up!

As a starter, for next 24 hours make a note of everything that you have not been willing to receive and everything that you are willing to receive (with gratitude and no barrier whatsoever)! If you receive something but it comes with an obligation to give back that's not true receiving! I have been doing this all day and I realized I wasn't willing to receive certain awareness about me. Well, I pushed down my walls and now I am, and there is more ease in my life!

Day 19

We will continue playing with "Receiving" today because this is such a vital element of vulnerability and this is one of the things that we don't do very well on this planet.

Open your awareness to receiving from things that you would never even dream of receiving from. Look at what it is to receive from nature, sunset, trees, insects, oceans, mountains, animals, nature spirits (fairies/gnomes/elves), photographs, paintings, art, buildings/architecture, etc. Receive from the furniture in your house, your mobile phone, your laptop, the food that you eat, the water you drink, books that you read, your car, vehicles out on the street, basically anything and everything that you interact with and find around you. Of course, continue receiving from people around you too.

WHAT ARE YOU WILLING TO RECEIVE, THAT OTHERS ARE NOT WILLING TO RECEIVE, THAT IF YOU WOULD BE OPEN TO RECEIVING IT, WOULD CREATE YOUR LIFE THE WAY YOU HAVE ALWAYS DESIRED?

What does it look like to receive from things you would never ever receive from?

What contribution can every molecule be to your life?

What contribution are these things being to you already that you are not acknowledging?

How does your life expand in the next 24 hours if you are willing to receive from every single teeny tiny molecule of energy and consciousness of this universe you are part of?

How many barriers melt away with ease when you do this?

Do those barriers even exist when you open up to this level of receiving?

Have you ever perceived the depth of receiving that is possible for you?

Are you willing to go beyond what you can fathom, when it comes to receiving?

I just started receiving from these words that are flowing out and getting written here and my body is vibrating with the energy of these words as I type. Did I ever know that was possible? Not until this moment!

Day 20

TIME TO LET GO!

We all do resistance. I get it! Today look at what/who is it in your life that you are resisting? What are you holding onto that you are unwilling to let go of?

Anything that you hold on to and not willing to let go, limits you and controls your life.

What would my life be like if I chose to let go of this?

How would I show up differently if I didn't hold on to this resistance anymore and chose to let it go?

Please know, letting go is a choice. You don't have to do it with force. You can be kind to yourself and allow the barriers to dissolve, or walk through it slowly till it has no effect on you anymore.

Day 21

Trust yourself today, no matter what!

Are you willing to let go of all the barriers you have to trusting you completely? What if you trusted every awareness that you have today, 1000 percent? And what if you could do this for your entire life?

Is there anything currently in your life that is sticky, something you are looking to get clarity on, resolve? What if you take a moment today, lower all your barriers to this person/situation and ask - what is it that you already know here that you are not willing to acknowledge? If you receive this awareness, what changes will that create in your life?

Let go of all the barriers of doubt that you have and just trust, trust and trust. No matter how illogical, impractical or unrealistic it appears. No matter who says what. What if today is the day where you don't deny your 'knowing' even once?

What difference would trusting YOU create in your life today?

Day 22

Vulnerability with Your Business

If you don't own a business you can do this with any job/project you are working on.

Lower your barriers to your business and be willing to

receive the awareness from it. What contribution can you be to your business?

What contribution can you receive from it?

How many defenses and blocks to knowing and receiving what your business requires and is asking for, do you have?

Do you have resistance to success of your business? Or resistance to failure? Are you willing to let go of it today?

Do you "need" your business or do you "desire" it? Where have you made your business a necessity rather than a choice?

If you were to be vulnerable with your business/career/ project what would you choose differently?

How would your business/project/career grow? What else is possible?!

I've noticed that the more I am vulnerable with my business, I am willing to be aware of the future of my business and what I choose with my business keeps changing. There is no fixed business plan, it seems to change every moment based on what works at that moment and it is opening up new possibilities, beyond what I could have imagined!

Day 23

Continue to play with vulnerability with business today. One of the key elements of a business is your clients/ customers/end users. How vulnerable are you with your clients? Have you ever considered it?

Have you noticed what gets created when you drop your barriers while you interact with your clients/consumers?

Do you have a point of view that you have to see every client who calls you or wants to work with you?

Are you willing to lose your clients and have no judgments about it?

Have you ever asked what kind of clients/customers/end users do you like to play with, in your business? What kind of clients would be fun for you and bring joy to your life?

I wonder what awesomeness you can create with your job/business when you choose to be more vulnerable with your clients/customers?

Day 24
Vulnerability as the Source Point of Creation of Everything

One of the things I have been doing for the last couple of months is to explore how vulnerability can be the source of creations. I see how differently I am creating things in my life and how much more successful, joyful and fun they are! What if everything that you create from today, you use vulnerability as the source and foundation for it?

How different would your creations be then?

Would you continue to choose what you are choosing or would you choose something different?

Remember – you are creating YOU every single day as well. So I wonder how different would YOU be?!

How many barriers do you have for creating things in your life?

How many creations are whispering into your awareness,

waiting out there, wanting to be created but you are not listening because you have confined yourself in your boundaries of beliefs?

How many of these creations are you avoiding so that you don't feel uncomfortable?

And how many creations don't want to be manifested because NOW is not the time, they are for the future, but you are still forcing it, by making them a "necessity"?

Play with this today and see what shows up.

Day 25

One of the things I struggled with all my life is the need for approval from people and the need to please everyone around me so that people think I am a 'nice girl' and to get everyone to like me! Did it work? NO WAY! I had this barrier up all my life because I hated receiving rejection, I hated hearing NO from people. So I would stretch way beyond to do things I disliked totally simply because I couldn't say NO to people and I couldn't hear NO from them. And this changed when I started using the tools of Access Consciousness® and even more when I started playing with vulnerability.

I also realized I was not asking for enough because I thought I would hear a NO. So I had stopped asking for things in my life! Remember: Ask and You shall Receive. If you don't ask, you don't receive! How much of your receiving do you cut off by not asking in the first place as you have already concluded that you will hear a NO or you dislike hearing a NO?

How many of you here can relate to this? Would you like to change it now?

1. Practice saying NO today – to those things which you would have said YES to, because you want to please people or get their approval. Do this until you have the ease to say NO to something that doesn't work for you.

2. Practice receiving NOs from people. Ask people for things you would never ask for! The challenge is to receive a NO and receive it with ease. You can ask someone can I have your car? Will you give me a million dollars? Can I have your shoes? Will you sponsor my vacation? It's fun!

When I started asking things, I was surprised to see people said YES to many things that I thought I'd get a NO for. As the universal law goes, Ask and you shall receive. You won't receive things unless you ask for it! Every time someone says NO, see if your defenses goes up, lower it down until you can receive the "NO" easily.

You will be amazed to see what this exercise can create for YOU, if you really play with it. Have fun!

Day 26

FLOW YOUR CREATIVITY

Each one of us is creative and brilliant in our own unique way. How many of us truly acknowledge this, tap into this creativity and allow it to show up in the world?

Today, lower all the barriers that you have to your ideas, your creative flow. What is it that you aware of that you are pretending not to know?

How many ideas and sparks of creativity are currently shining in your space and you are not willing to even notice? Spend a few minutes lowering all the walls you have created to these ideas and creative projects that are waiting to be created through you. Note them all down in a book, without having to think about how, where, what, when etc. You can start maintaining a book of ideas. If you get overwhelmed with loads of ideas flowing, ask a question if it is for the present. Few of them maybe for the future, so you don't have to work on them now but you want to remember them. Acknowledge them all and receive what this creative flow has to contribute to your life.

Take action on those that want to be created right now.

The more you listen and receive, the more you trust yourself, the more ideas will flow for you to discover.

Day 27

I have mentioned before that I have been lucky enough to come across a few people who have truly embraced vulnerability. One of the key things I have seen in all of them is the kindness, gentleness and softness they have with themselves and with every single person they interact with, no matter how annoying that person may be! Their body reflects this in totality, every molecule of their body is full of kindness and gentleness and just a hug from them can change your life and contribute to your body!

I have been asking and demanding from me to be all of this. But I often notice that the person I am unkind to, the most, is ME. Whether it is to judge me or not take time out to nurture my body or say yes to something that is not honoring of me.

What if you spend the next 24 hours being extremely kind and gentle to yourself and to your sweet body AND being that kindness and gentleness with every single person you interact with? What if the kindness you be can change the world?

As Dain Heer says, no one can take away the kindness you are or diminish your capacities. Even if you think your kindness has disappeared and you have become 'tough' because of circumstances in your life, please remember you have just hidden it and it is not lost. What if you can bring that kindness you were as a kid?

What if you being YOU without any barriers and full of kindness and gentleness can change people around you? Are you willing to be that GIFT to you and to others and to this planet?

Day 28

CHANGING THE WORLD BY EMBRACING VULNERABILITY

Did you know that by choosing to be vulnerable you can actually change the world? For every wall/barrier that you let go you are showing the people around you that it is actually possible and it gives them the permission to let go of it too; so you are inspiring people to let go of their own barriers. What a huge gift you can be to this planet by choosing more of this!

What if every wall/barrier that you have created in your life is to show the world that they can undo and unlock them and let it go? Have you ever thought about that? Can you acknowledge this capacity you have?

When you are willing to let your barriers go it tells people that they can do it too and it gets easier! How does it get better than that?

What are the different ways you have contributed to changing the world, been a gift to people around you by choosing to let go of your barriers, judgments and being more vulnerable over the past 1 month?

Can you be grateful for YOU today for choosing this challenge and being the catalyst of change that this world requires and desires? Would you like to explore this today?

Day 29

As a result of doing this challenge for 28 days non-stop I feel extremely spacey today but in a good way. Lots of joy, ease, peace and space everywhere. Is anyone else feeling this way?

I am very grateful for myself today and celebrating ME, for having chosen this for an entire month and for having committed to my life to create what I desire. Are you being grateful for you?

In the past 28 days, things that were not working for me have collapsed; people who were not honoring of me have drifted away; new creations have emerged; and new people who are contributing to my life have shown up! Did I ask for this directly? NO, but I did ask for vulnerability and made a demand to choose it every single day, which allowed all of this to show up! Change will never look the way you expect it to, remember?

Take time to recognize and acknowledge the changes that have already shown up in your life for the past 28 days. Time to be grateful!

Day 30

It is day 30 today and we are at the end of this challenge and I'd love to see at it as the beginning of something greater. I hope you had as much fun as I did, playing with the tools for an entire month. Even though this challenge stops here, you still carry the energy of these 30 days with you with whatever you be and create in your life. What if it is now easier to embrace vulnerability than before?

Will you please acknowledge and receive everything that has changed for you in these 30 days, no matter how insignificant you have decided it is?

What if this is the starting point you required towards being more of you, to be more authentic and to get out of the safety of your comfort zone, to be vulnerable and start creating your life the way you desire? Is now the time to choose to be truly vulnerable and step out into the world, show up as you are and use all the tools that we played with here for one entire month?!

If you choose to embrace the brilliance that you are, what can you create in and as your life going forward?

What capacities of you can you unlock and choose right now?

The Man who Inspired Me

Dr. Dain Heer, author, speaker and co-creator of Access Consciousness®, has a very special place in my heart. His book *"Being You, Changing the World"* was an invitation for me to explore more of Access Consciousness®, which transformed my life, to say the least. He has been a huge inspiration and invitation for me to choose not just vulnerability but to choose more of ME and step into my greatness. He is someone who showed me a different way of being, which I never knew was possible. It is very interesting that someone can change your entire life just by the vulnerability that they embrace and that's the gift he hs been for me. This book wouldn't have been written if not for him embodying vulnerability and showing me that it is actually possible!

I had the pleasure of meeting Dain and Gary in person three years ago at my first Access Facilitators class in Australia. Since then, over the years I've seen Dain Heer transform exponentially and more so in the past six months, where I have seen him choose more of his greatness, potency and the magic that he is.

I speak mostly for myself here but I have no doubt that thousands of people will echo what I have to share.

Dain Heer is magical, to say the least. He is an incredible healer, dynamic speaker and a facilitator extraordinaire. He is kindness, gentleness, grace, beauty and awesomeness personified. Honestly, I haven't come across another man in my life (other than my husband) who is like him, with a huge amount of caring, kindness and vulnerability that oozes out of every pore of his body and being. He is remarkably different than anyone else I have met so far. Just being in his presence or his warm caring hug can melt your world and change your entire reality, if you are willing to receive it. Been there, experienced it, so I vouch for that! It's only when I met him personally, attended several of his classes and saw him facilitate change in thousands of people's lives by just being him, that I truly understood what "Being You, Changing the World" looks like. He is living that every moment. It's a rarity these days to find someone who walks their talk.

I noticed how his space of no judgment and vulnerability made me feel instantly included in his world. He literally has no barriers around him and is willing to gift and receive from everyone around. When he looks at you with his enticing eyes of no judgments, you begin to see you; the true YOU that exists behind all the masks and pretences that you have created. That is such an amazing capacity of his that very few people in this world have. For the first time in my life I was able to receive more of myself in this process.

His sweetness, softness, kindness and vulnerability makes him extremely attractive and charming, obviously! When I saw all of that and the way he had chosen to step into his magic and potency, I knew I wanted to have and be everything that he was having and being. I made a demand to do

166

whatever it takes to have it all. Finally, someone had showed me what it is like to be vulnerable and what it can create and change in the world. It's only because I had seen it in him, I knew it was possible. From that moment I chose to lower my barriers, to myself and everyone & everything around me, every single day. In just a couple of months of doing this, my life had transformed. There was more joy and ease in my life and more possibilities opening up effortlessly which I had never even imagined. But little did I acknowledge that it was because of the choices and demand I had made. I obviously expected it to look very different. As Dain Heer always says "change never looks or feels the way you think it is going to"! So I was clearly not willing to receive it all and it's funny that I kept judging myself for not being vulnerable and that too fast enough. I always like to have things instantly, right now or even better, I'd like it yesterday!

I heard Gary and Dain say that "It's only because you have it within you that you can acknowledge it in others". It got me pondering. If I admire what I admire in Dain, does it mean I have it within me too? When I asked Dain Heer about this in a class few months back, he said "*What you admire in somebody else is what you already are that you are not allowing yourself to be or what you are not allowing yourself to know that you be*". He said what I admire in him, he also sees it in me. He continued to acknowledge some of the gifts and capacities that I have, without trying to validate me. I stood there like a dog watching television, trying to let it in to the best of my ability, wondering what the heck is he talking about?! It sounded bizarre to me and way beyond my comprehension that I was being all of what he acknowledged about me. One of the reasons being, I had never once considered in my life that I had any gifts or capacities whatsoever! That facade was now being shattered thanks to the space of genuineness and kindness he was being. I had to go back home, push down my barriers completely and listen to our conversation at least 50 times before I could receive it all.

Only then I noticed how amazingly he had invited me to see the gift that I am, hidden underneath the self I usually present to this world. I would have probably never seen this, if not for him bringing it to my awareness and it transformed my life, to say the least. I was in tears for weeks after that as I received more and more of what he had acknowledged about me and let it sink in, finding more of my real self in the process. I felt raw and open and I could perceive all my barriers melt away and dissolve. For the first time I could feel what it was like to be vulnerable with myself.

There are times when you know something different and greater is possible for you, beyond cognition and what is conceivable in this reality and you are only aware of the subtle wisps of that energy but you have no idea how to get it, do it, be it or have it. All you know is that you desire it and you are very much asking for it. Then someone as amazing as Dain Heer walks into your life and is being the energy that matches it so you get to see it in action, contributes to your life in ways that you had never imagined, acknowledges certain things about you and says exactly those things required to swing open the doorways for you to be able to access those greater possibilities in your life, giving access to more of YOU in the process! I am extremely grateful for him and consider myself very lucky to have been in his presence.

He has always inspired me to be greater and is one of those people who has had my back in this journey, no matter where he is in the world. This is another one of the gifts that he has. I've never felt the need to be physically in front of him or in a class or email or text him to ask for something. All I have to do is ask and I receive, all of it energetically and effortlessly.

Dain Heer continues to be an inspiration for me every day and shows me a completely different level of his capacities every single time I see him and it literally blows my mind. I am learning what it is like to out-create myself, by seeing him do it so brilliantly. This has helped me in unlocking and unleashing my talents, abilities and gifts that I have hidden for way too long and I end up surprising myself more often than not, when I discover them!

Thank you Dr. Dain, for being YOU and for being so remarkably brilliant, magical and awesome. Thank you for showing me a different way of being. Thank you for helping me to open up to energies that I knew existed but wasn't able to receive them before. Thank you for the gift that you have been for me and everyone else in this world. It amazes me to see how you keep gifting to all of us without giving up on us even if we have given up on ourselves! This world needs more people like you and the world is definitely a better place because of you. Thank you for BEING!

Words always fall short whenever I want to express how truly, deeply and extremely grateful I am for you. My gratitude for you goes way beyond what words can convey and I know you know that anyway!

Epilogue

Sharing my stories and learnings and going through this journey of vulnerability together with you has been one of my most amazing experiences so far. I am very grateful for you for choosing to come along with me on this adventurous and transformational journey. Thank you for the gift that you are to me, to everyone in your life and to this planet!

I see this not as an end, but a beginning of something greater. I know what I've discovered about vulnerability is just a tip of the iceberg and there is a lot more available for me and all of us to explore and choose. I am excited to continue seeking on this inward journey and discover how much more of me I can unleash, unlock and unveil.

What would it take for more of us to create ourselves, our business, our finances, our body, our relationships and our entire life with a vulnerable presence, every moment?

Imagine, if every single one of us chooses to be more authentic, willing to say what we know (through writing, speaking, singing, dancing, painting etc), bring our creations into this world without any judgments, be comfortable in asking for what we want from people around us, receive more of everything, be as powerful as we are, and have no barriers whatsoever, how different will this world be? If each and every person on this planet embodied vulnerability, caring, kindness, softness, gentleness to themselves and others, how different will this world be? Can you get the energy of it right now? Isn't it exciting to know a possibility exists to live in a world full of love, laughter, joy and oneness? That's my target, to contribute, in my own way, towards creating a world like that.

I love choosing to be more vulnerable because I see people around me change as I choose more of it. It gives me a great opportunity for personal growth while I let people into my world and allow them to interact with my exposed true self. When you are authentic, it encourages people around you to be authentic too. When I talk about my personal experiences in my classes, in private sessions, on social media or my blog, it has a greater impact, builds a deeper connection with people reading it and inspires them to choose something different too.

When you pour your heart out and share from a space of vulnerability, looking at what you have chosen, your audience know it is possible for them to choose it too, in their lives. That's how you become an invitation and inspiration for people to create something greater for themselves. As Dain Heer says, "You being more of YOU, changes the world."

Please know that it is not about making vulnerability a "need". When you make something a necessity in your life, you have judgments associated with it, whether you are being it or not. It takes fun out of the equation. What if instead of the need to be vulnerable, you desire it? When you desire something, you don't have an expectation of how and when it should show up, there is no timeline attached and you are fine if it shows up and fine if it doesn't. There is total freedom and choice.

"Being vulnerable starts with choice."

What else is possible now that we have not yet considered?

About the Author

PRATIMA NAGARAJ

Pratima Nagaraj is an internationally known facilitator with the dynamic body of energy transformational work-Access Consciousness®. She travels the world facilitating classes and sessions that empower people to make choices to shift and transform any area of their life that is not working for them. Pratima is known for her awareness, allowance and ease of facilitation. She is also a Clinical Hypnotherapist, certified with the board of National Guild of Hypnotists, Past Life Regression Specialist, EFT practitioner, Reiki Master and Pranic Healer. Every modality she has learnt has contributed to her personal journey of transformation.

Prior to this, Pratima has worked in the corporate world for six years in multinational organizations in the Information

Technology industry. She has an Engineering degree and a Masters degree in Business Administration. It has been an amazing and adventurous journey of transformation for her from being a Business Analyst to becoming a Hypnotherapist and a facilitator of consciousness.

Pratima has personally used the tools of Access Consciousness for many years to radically transform her business, health, financial reality and relationships. Her level of awareness of people and the spirit world is phenomenal and she uses this with ease to facilitate her clients. People who have attended her classes acknowledge that her dynamic facilitation with the space of no judgement, kindness and vulnerability has been a catalyst for them to choose change in their lives. She has also created a successful 6-figure income business in less than five years and now uses her background from business and experience of the corporate world along with the tools of Access Consciousness® to coach aspiring entrepreneurs, small and medium sized organizations to transform their businesses, increase income and add more fun and joy to it. Her target is to spread more awareness and consciousness in this world and invite people to create a different reality for themselves through kindness, awareness, allowance and choice.

You can know more about her and her work at www.pratimanagaraj.com.